D0597045

Gertrude Stein
An Annotated Critical Bibliography

Gertrude Stein

An Annotated Critical Bibliography

Maureen R. Liston

The Kent State University Press

The Serif Series: Number 35
Bibliographies and Checklists

Dean H. Keller, General Editor
Kent State University

Library of Congress Cataloging in Publication Data

Liston, Maureen R
    Gertrude Stein.

    (The Serif series, bibliographies and checklists; no. 35)
    Includes indexes.
    1. Stein, Gertrude, 1874-1946—Bibliography.
I. Series.
Z8838.9.L57   [PS3537.T323]   016.818′5′209
ISBN 0-87338-221-8   78-21971

Copyright© 1979 by The Kent State University Press,
    Kent, Ohio 44242
All rights reserved
Library of Congress Catalog Card Number: 78-21971
ISBN: 0-87338-221-8
Manufactured in the United States of America

Für Inge, die Katze und Max

Contents

Contents

Contents

x   **Contents**

Introduction

Gertrude Stein's first book, *Three Lives*, was published on 30 July 1909, and the first reviews appeared in December. In the decades that followed, Stein's writings were to receive increasing critical attention and, as this checklist demonstrates, there now exists a substantial body of secondary literature on Stein, her work, and her celebrated Paris salon. Unhappily, much of it is marred by insufficient research, slovenly scholarship, cattiness, misquotations, plagiarism, and an inexcusable lack of familiarity with the primary literature. There have been the rare understanding review, the elucidating article and, beginning in the 1960s, the insightful and scholarly study, but the critical literature can be more accurately appraised with negativisms. Stein herself realized the danger of such misrepresentations, for she commented "that other people's writings about her writing did her more harm than her own writing." Robert Bartlett Haas complements that judgment in noting that "Gertrude Stein has not always been fortunate in her biographers . . . or her explainers, and only a handful of essays . . . come up to my notion of what illuminates the character of Gertrude Stein's contribution." (See I-B-iii-70, Preface.)

Although this checklist is selective rather than complete, I have attempted to present the different critical approaches to Stein's work, the literary influences she had, and other artists' responses to her. These views tend to be repetitious and I have chosen to exclude numerous articles and books in order to produce a research tool both practical and usable for critic and student.

For this reason, only some *Time* and *Newsweek* articles are listed as examples of these magazines' approach to book reviews, which is summarization. Announcements of publication are not included; samples of foreign language articles are. The checklist covers 1909 through early 1978, and, although research has been thorough, I assume important critical articles from 1975-1978 might be missing, due to lack of bibliographic information for those years. I have attempted to examine only first editions of all books—later reprints or editions were not taken into consideration—and have seen everything listed here except for those manuscripts and typescripts housed in Bancroft Library, Berkeley, California.

The checklist is not designed for a Stein neophyte. The methodology adapted is based on the assumption that the user has some acquaintance with Gertrude Stein.

Robert A. Wilson writes that the success or failure of a bibliography depends upon contributions by many people (I-A-i-7). This checklist developed through the support and interest of Prof. Dr. David D. Galloway (Ruhr-Universität Bochum, West Germany), who also read several drafts of an earlier form of the present work and offered constructive criticism. I am indebted to him for his professional advice and for his long friendship. Prof. Dr. Ulrich Suerbaum also offered criticisms on an earlier version, for which I am grateful.

Research was carried out in the United States, in Germany and in England. Staffs of the following libraries have been generous with time and help: Kansas City, Missouri, Public Library; Cleveland, Ohio, Public Library; Freiburger Library, Case Western Reserve University, Cleveland, Ohio; New York Public Library; The British Museum; Exeter University Library; Universitätsbibliothek, Ruhr-Universität Bochum. It was only after the completion of this checklist that I was able to use the Beinecke Library, Yale University, New Haven, Connecticut. The Gertrude Stein Collection includes innumerable articles—critical, biographical and memorial—on Stein. Among these is a collection of review clippings from the Romeike Agency; these contain the name of the newspaper and the date of publication, but rarely include pagination. The Beinecke is the most pleasant library I have worked in, and the critic who wishes to study Stein's critical reception will find an extraordinary amount of information there.

I owe a great deal of thanks to those friends and acquaintances who were always on the lookout for articles, who helped with proofreading, indices and photocopying, and who always offered support. The Lehrstuhl für Amerikanistik, Englisches Seminar, Ruhr-Universität Bochum, allowed me a very generous amount of time to complete this work.

For the errors that surely exist I alone am responsible; I would appreciate corrections and addenda from readers.

MRL

I. Bibliographical and Biographical Material

A. Bibliographies

i. Books

1. Firmage, George James. *A Checklist of the Published Writings of Gertrude Stein*. Amherst: University of Massachusetts Press, 1954.

   Only eight pages long, Firmage's *Checklist* has been superseded by more recent bibliographies.

2. Gerstenberger, Donna and George Hendrick. *The American Novel: A Checklist of Twentieth Century Criticism on Novels Written Since 1789. Volume I: 1789-1959. Volume II: Criticism Written 1960-1968.* Chicago: Swallow, 1961 and 1970.

   The information on Stein in Volume I is skimpy. Volume II attributes Michael J. Hoffman's articles to Frederick J. Hoffman.

3. Gotham Book Mart. Gertrude Stein. Catalog 1964.

   "More Laurels for our Gertrude," by Carl Van Vechten, appears at the beginning of the Catalog (pp. iii-iv?). The Catalog is divided into eight sections: books by Stein; autographed materials and photographs; Stein's contributions to books and pamphlets; and to magazines; miscellanea; books about Stein; magazine articles on Stein and her work; recordings and music.

1

4. Haas, Robert Bartlett and Donald Clifford Gallup, comps. *A Catalogue of the Published and Unpublished Writings of Gertrude Stein*. New Haven: Yale University Library, 1941.

This catalog covers the Yale exhibition from 22 February to 29 March 1941. It contains: "Books and Pamphlets by Gertrude Stein" (1898-1941); "Books and Pamphlets with Contributions from Gertrude Stein" (1914-1939); "A Chronological List of the Published and Unpublished Writings of Gertrude Stein" (1904-1940). The latter is based on the Stein *transition* bibliography, updated (see I-A-ii-3). The first two sections contain bibliographical information of interest to book collectors. Haas and Gallup must be supplemented by the much more recent II-A-2.

5. Sawyer, Julian. *Gertrude Stein: A Bibliography*. New York: Arrow Edition, 1940.

This bibliography—outdated by I-A-i-7—contains a lengthy preface, "Descriptions of Gertrude Stein," pp. 13-30; Sawyer attempts to elucidate Stein's published works but does not succeed. He includes Stein's references to her various publications, an idea later to be adopted and expanded by Richard Bridgman in "Appendix D. Index of the Names and Titles Mentioned in *The Autobiography of Alice B. Toklas, Lectures in America,* and *Everybody's Autobiography*," *Gertrude Stein in Pieces* (II-A-2). The bibliography includes books, brochures, contributions to books and magazines, music and records, and miscellanea.

6. Schwartz, Harry W. *Checklists of Twentieth Century Authors*. Third Series. Milwaukee: Casanova Booksellers, 1935.

Schwartz includes Frank Harris, Robert Nathan, Erskine Caldwell, A. Edward Newton, and Gertrude Stein (pp. 18-19). He lists only books and monographs; among other things, the Plain Edition books are not listed in chronological order.

7. Wilson, Robert A., comp. *Gertrude Stein: A Bibliography.*
   New York: Phoenix Bookshop, 1974.
     The contents are as follows: A. "Books and Pamphlets by
   Gertrude Stein"; B. "Books and Pamphlets with Contributions
   by Gertrude Stein"; C. "Contributions to Periodicals"; D.
   "Translations into Foreign Languages of Works by Gertrude
   Stein"; E. "Musical Settings of Works by Gertrude Stein"; F.
   "Recordings of Gertrude Stein's Works"; G. "Ephemera and
   Miscellanea"; H. "The Published Works of Alice B. Toklas";
   I. "A Book Attributed to Gertrude Stein"; J. "Selected List of
   Critical and Biographical Materials about Gertrude Stein."
   Despite some inaccuracies, Wilson's bibliography is the most
   complete primary bibliography of Stein.

ii. Articles

1. Sawyer, Julian. "Gertrude Stein: A Checklist
   Comprising Critical and Miscellaneous Writings
   about Her Work, Life, Personality from 1913-1942."
   Bulletin of Bibliography, 17 (January-April 1943),
   211-12; 18 (May-August 1943), 11-13.
2. ———. "Gertrude Stein: A Bibliography, 1941-48."
   Bulletin of Bibliography, 19 (May-August, September-
   December 1948), 152-56 and 183-87.
3. Stein, Gertrude. "Bibliography." *transition,* 3
   February 1929), 47-55.
     This bibliography was compiled by Stein on her writings
   from 1904 until 1929. Robert Bartlett Haas and Donald Gallup
   state that Stein's "was not yet reliable from the technical
   bibliographer's point of view" (I-A-i-4).

   See also Richard Bridgman's "Selected
   Bibliography" (in II-A-2), which lists the "Principal
   Volumes and Collections of Gertrude Stein," and
   "Appendix C. Key to the *Yale Catalogue,* Part 4."

B. Biographies

i. Biographies and Memoirs of Gertrude Stein (including books and typescripts)

1. Barlow, Samuel L. M. "Ave dione: A tribute." Typescript at Beinecke Library, Yale Collection of American Literature, Yale University.

   Barlow waited over thirty years before writing his recollections of a trip with Gertrude Stein and Alice B. Toklas through Provence in 1918. Besides this 16-page carbon copy, Yale also holds three pages of an earlier version, "Tour of Provence with Miss Stein and Miss Toklas."

2. Brinnin, John Malcolm. *The Third Rose: Gertrude Stein and Her World.* Boston: Atlantic, Little, Brown, 1959.

   Brinnin's was the most complete and readable of the early Stein biographies. Despite factual errors and lack of annotation, Brinnin managed to bring life to the history of a myth and milieu in a scholarly manner; W. G. Rogers's (I-B-i-11) had simply been the remembrance of a friend, and Elizabeth Sprigge's (I-B-i-16) reasons for writing about Stein were and are unclear. James Mellow's new biography (I-B-i-9) of Stein is more complete and factually more accurate, but Brinnin's must be historically appreciated as the first detailed biography in which literary criticism, art history, and social history were intertwined, one which was not to replaced for 15 years.

3. Burnett, Avis. *Gertrude Stein.* New York: Atheneum, 1972.

   Several biographies were published after the 1970 Museum of Modern Art's "Four Americans in Paris." Burnett's is comparable in content and worth to the others, excepting James Mellow's (I-B-i-9). Burnett has created dialogs to flesh out the bare biographical facts.

4

4. Faÿ, Bernard. *Les Précieux*. Paris: Librarie
   Académique Perrin, 1966.

   Section VI (pp. 137-69) is "Le Parfum d'une Rose," a memory
   and description of Gertrude Stein. In 1924 Faÿ met Stein
   and Alice B. Toklas. This essay is not only about them, but
   also of the others (Ernest Hemingway, Sherwood Anderson,
   et al.) who met at Rue de Fleurus. There are some biographical
   errors. He translates sections of *Paris France*, and includes
   comments on *Three Lives, Making of Americans* (for which he wrote a
   preface), *Autobiography of Alice B. Toklas* and *Brewsie and Willie*.

   "En français elle montrait plus de verve, grâce à l'emploi,
   inconscient, de mots, trop forts pour ce qu'elle désirait
   exprimer. En anglais, elle avait plus de finesse et d'humour,
   car elle connaissait avec une précision insolite la signification
   des mots, leur portée, leur résonance. Je commençais à
   connaître l'anglais suffisament pour apprécier son adresse,
   en jouir et chercher à en profiter."

   "Elle le faisait rondement; et commençait par me rappeler
   que, du côté de sa mère, elle descendait d'une dynastie de
   rabbins distingués."

5. Gallup, Donald, ed. *The Flowers of Friendship: Letters
   Written to Gretrude Stein*. New York: Knopf,
   1953.

   This is a sampling of the letters written Gertrude Stein.
   See II-F-iii.

6. Greenfeld, Howard. *Gertrude Stein: A Biography*. New
   York: Crown, 1973.

   Greenfeld's is an inadequate retelling of other biographies.
   There are some inaccuracies.

7. Hobhouse, Janet. *Everybody Who Was Anybody: A Biography of Gertrude Stein*. New York: Putnam, 1975.

   The photographs used are good, but the biography as a whole is superficial. Hobhouse draws on the Stein Notebooks presented by Leon Katz in his dissertation (II-B-13) and in *Fernhurst, Q.E.D., and Other Early Writings* to write more explicitly about Stein's lesbianism.

8. Lachman, Arthur. "Gertrude Stein As I Knew Her." Typescript at Yale Collection of American Literature.

   Lachman knew Stein at Harvard. His memoir describes her appearance, their Saturday and Sunday meetings, and makes some comments about her developments since her Harvard days.

9. Mellow, James R. *Charmed Circle: Gertrude Stein and Company*. New York: Praeger, 1974.

   Mellow's is the definitive biography of Gertrude Stein. His is highly researched yet readable, factually the most accurate and the most complete. Although Mellow states in the "Acknowledgments" that he "had no ambitions about writing a 'definitive' life," he has done just that. Mellow's biography is an invaluable tool for those interested in Stein.

10. Rather, Lois. *Gertrude Stein and California*. Oakland, California: The Rather Press, 1974.

    Only 130 copies of Rather's *Gertrude Stein* were printed. Despite errors in punctuation and grammar, this provides the best background on Stein's youth; Rather includes much information on Oakland in the 1880s, and uses Annette Rosenshine (I-B-ii-76), Roland Duncan (I-B-iii-35), Harriet Levy (I-B-ii-61), and Amelia Keyser's diaries. The book includes such information as that Stein had measles in mid-February 1881; in 1880 the Steins stayed in a hotel, then moved to a furnished house for $55-a-month; Amelia ran the household on $300 given her by Dan; on 28 April 1881 the Steins moved to the Stratton farm, where they lived for four

years. Rather quotes *Making of Americans* for childhood
information.

Rather includes detailed information on Stein's 1935
California visit. There are some textual and factual errors:
she credits Francis Rose's *Vogue* article (I-B-iii-71) with
first publishing "Pussy" and "Lovey," for instance.
Some questions are raised: did Stein wear pince-nez? Did
she plan to return to the United States in the fall of 1946?

Despite its many inaccuracies and errors, Rather's book
provides invaluable background information on Stein's
childhood.

11. Rogers, W. G. *When This You See Remember Me: Gertrude
Stein in Person*. New York: Rinehart, 1948.

Roger's book is more an *in memoriam* than a biography. He
considers *Three Lives* and *Tender Buttons* Stein's "prime
contribution to modern letters." *When This You See* includes
some defense of Stein, but it is neither logical nor convincing.
Toklas and Stein are referred to as the "perfect pair, each
supplying what the other lacked. . . ." Rogers attempts to
explain *The Making of Americans* and *Four Saints in Three
Acts* ("the landscape itself").

As a sample of Roger's defense, he writes that if people
had known Stein personally, she would have turned them to
her books.

The worthwhile part of this book is Roger's recollection
and narration of those phases of Alice and Gertrude's life
during which he was with them.

12. ———. *Gertrude Stein Is Gertrude Stein Is Gertrude
Stein: Her Life and Work*. New York: Crowell, 1973.

This is one of a series of "Women in America," published
by Crowell for juveniles. Both Rogers and Ellen Wilson
(I-B-i-23) identify the people in the same family portrait (ca.
1880) differently from any of Stein's other biographers.

13. Simon, Linda, ed. *Gertrude Stein: A Composite Portrait.*
New York: Avon Books, 1974.

Simon's book is an anthology of reminiscences of Stein, all
of which are by very well known people: Alice B. Toklas, Pablo
Picasso, Sylvia Beach, Sherwood Anderson, Ernest Hemingway,
Edith Sitwell, Virgil Thomson, to name but a few.

Simon is "working on a new book about Alice B. Toklas."
(See following entry.) If it contains the same difficulties as *Gertrude
Stein*, its usefulness will be limited. *Gertrude Stein* is not only
filled with proofreading errors, but also lacks footnotes and a
bibliography. Its one positive point—a collection of oft-referred
to but difficult to find pieces on Stein—is thus radically negated.

14. Simon, Linda. *The Biography of Alice B. Toklas.* New
York: Doubleday, 1977.

Simon's biography leaves much to be desired. Despite
bringing together materials usually only referred to—Harriet
Levy (I-B-ii-61) and Annette Rosenshine (I-B-ii-76), for
instance—there is less focus on Toklas than one would
desire. The opening chapters, pre-Stein, are interesting, and
the appendix "An Annotated Gertrude Stein" "is meant to
supplement Richard Bridgman's dissection of Gertrude Stein
into pieces. . . ."

15. Sorell, Walter. "Gertrude Stein: A Mind Is a Mind
Is a Mind," in *Three Women: Lives of Sex and Genius.*
New York: Bobbs-Merrill, 1975. Pp. 71-128.

Very superficial.

16. Sprigge, Elizabeth. *Gertrude Stein: Her Life and Work.*
London: Hamish Hamilton, 1957.

The importance of this book, the first biography of Stein,
has diminished over the years. In fact, the publication two
years later of Brinnin's *The Third Rose* (I-B-i-2) replaced
Sprigge's book in the amount and in the presentation of
information. The endless bits of facts and dates are made
neither exciting nor interesting by Sprigge (although this may
be a prejudice against a very British style). She does attempt
to provide a background for Stein's works, but is writing more
of a chatty biography than a literary criticism. Sprigge fails to
show the importance of much of the information she presents.

17. Steward, Samuel M., ed. *Dear Sammy: Letters from Gertrude Stein and Alice B. Toklas*. With a "Memoir" by Samuel M. Steward. Boston: Houghton Mifflin, 1977.

> The memoir runs from pp. 1-117 and, although clearly based on fact, tends frequently towards the unbelievable. Some of the conversations seem too good to be true, a mixture of Gertrude Stein's many books, and Steward appears more interested in filling in blanks in his autobiography than in telling about his experiences with Stein and Alice B. Toklas. The letters, pp. 119-245, and the photographs are more valuable.

18. Toklas, Alice B. *The Alice B. Toklas Cookbook*. New York: Harper, 1954.

> This, in fact, a first volume of Toklas's reminiscences, interspersed with recipes. It is much chattier than her *What Is Remembered* (I-B-i-20).

19. ———. *Aromas and Flavors of Past and Present*. New York: Harper, 1958.

20. ———. *What Is Remembered*. New York: Holt, Rinehart and Winston, 1963.

> The last chapter of Toklas's retelling of her life with Gertrude was not printed.

21. ———. *Staying on Alone: Letters of Alice B. Toklas*. Ed. Edward Burns. New York: Liveright, 1973.

> As with most books published by Liveright, *Staying on Alone* is filled with printer's/proofreader's errors. Burns's notes are fairly complete; he identifies so many references to people, places and manuscripts, however, that the few that fail become more noticeable.
>
> Toklas unfolds through her letters as a personality in her own right—an occurrence that seldom took place in writings by others. Her comments on life without Gertrude, on Stein's writings, on Stein's critics, on life with Stein are recorded in this selection. It is, of course, a must book for anyone interested in Stein, and for anyone interested in Paris 1910-1967.

22. White, Ray Lewis, ed. *Sherwood Anderson/Gertrude Stein: Correspondence and Personal Essays.* Chapel Hill: University of North Carolina Press, 1973.

23. Wilson, Ellen. *They Named Me Gertrude Stein.* New York: Farrar, Straus and Giroux, 1973.

     Wilson's is another post—"Four Americans in Paris" juvenile biography.

ii. Biographies, Memories and Criticisms of Others (books and typescripts)

Items under this heading provide background material or contain some mention of Gertrude Stein and Alice B. Toklas.

1. Aldrich, Mildred. *A Hilltop on the Marne.* Boston: Houghton Mifflin, 1915.

2. ————. *On the Edge of the War Zone.* Boston: Small, Maynard, 1917.

3. ————. *The Peak of the Load.* Small, Maynard, 1918.

4. ————. *When Johnny Comes Marching Home.* Boston: Small, Maynard and Co., 1919.

5. Anderson, Margaret. *My Thirty Years' War: An Autobiography.* New York: Covici, 1930.

     The autobiography of one of the founders of *Little Review* is filled with the people in Paris and New York (but mostly those in New York) in the 1920s. Pages 248-51 deal specifically with Gertrude Stein. "To me Gertrude Stein's style can be regarded as having two aspects. She has (1) a way of saying things which presents perfectly her special matter; she has (2) a way of repeating those things which detracts from her special manner."

Anderson states that *Making of Americans* would be improved "if every psychologically descriptive phrase were said once and once only." She does not rate Stein highly as a writer because of "a limitation to the 'vital singularity' she is capable of being interested in. . . . I feel she is full of homely important knowledge of simple vital people, lack of knowledge of many of the human masks, and I am not at all convinced that her imagination would respond to even a preliminary examination of what I would call significant singularity."

6. Anderson, Sherwood. *The Letters of Sherwood Anderson.* Ed. Howard Mumford Jones with Walter B. Rideout. Boston: Little, Brown, 1953.

   Letters contains eight letters to Gertrude Stein, together with many references to her, and an attempt by Anderson to combat B. F. Skinner (see II-C-30). Anderson's letter of introduction for Ernest Hemingway is also included.

7. ———. *Sherwood Anderson's Memoirs: A Critical Edition.* Ed. Ray Lewis White. Chapel Hill: University of North Carolina Press, 1969.

   Anderson did not write very fully of his relationship with Gertrude Stein. There are a few mentions, but not in the depth or breadth one would expect.

8. Antheil, George. *Bad Boy of Music.* New York: Doubleday, Doran, 1945.

   Antheil's biography is probably most important not because of what we learn of Stein (he mentions her name three times) but because he went to Europe shortly after the First World War and was acquainted with most of the people and places that were to play important roles in Stein's life.

9. Baker, Carlos. *Hemingway: The Writer As Artist.* Princeton: Princeton University Press, 1964.

10. ———. *Ernest Hemingway: A Life Story.* New York: Scribner's, 1969.

    Hemingway's relationship with Stein, her tutoring of him and their subsequent disagreements are downplayed.

11. Balmain, Pierre. *My Years and Seasons.* Trans. Edward Lanchberry with Gordon Young. London: Cassell, 1964.

    These are the reminiscences of the designer who knew Stein in Aix-les-Bains. They met during the Second World War, in 1941, and visited often in Biliguin [sic] near Beley [sic] and Culoz. Balmain includes part of Stein's *Vogue* article ("From Dark to Day," November 1945, p. 52) on him.

12. Barney, Natalie Clifford. "Gertrude Stein." *Aventures de l'esprit.* Paris: Emile-Paul, 1929. Pp. 231-43.

    Barney includes biographies and portraits of Romaine Brooks, Renée Vivien, Djuna Barnes, Elisabeth de Gramont, Colette, Stein, and others. Stein "a peut-être le plus influencé les jeunes écrivains de nos jours. . . ." Barney includes her translation of several passages from *The Making of Americans.*

13. ———. "Gertrude Stein." *Traits et portraits: suivi de l'amour defendu.* Mercure de France, 1963.

    Translation of II-D-13.

14. Beach, Sylvia, ed. *Les Années vingt: Les Écrivains américains à Paris et leur amis 1920-1930: Exposition du 11 mars au 25 avril 1959.* Paris: Centre Culturel Américain, 1959.

    Sylvia Beach, who was in charge of the organization of this exhibition, introduces the catalog. The exhibit included items from Shakespeare and Company, photographs, books, manuscripts—all sorts of literary memorabilia—from Paris 1920-30.

15. Beach, Sylvia. *Shakespeare and Company*. New York: Harcourt, Brace, 1959.

   Beach's memoirs are enjoyable, and provide very good background to the story of the American "expatriates." The chapter "Two Customers from the Rue de Fleurus" (pp. 27-29) describes Alice B. Toklas and Stein, and Beach also includes her version of Sherwood Anderson's first meeting with Stein and Toklas. Beach enjoyed Stein's writing, and got everything by Stein she could for the bookshop.

   Beach mentions that the "Plain Edition" was "attractively produced."

16. Beaton, Cecil. *Photobiography*. London: Oldhams Press, 1951.

   Beaton first photographed Alice B. Toklas and Stein when they went to London for *Wedding Bouquet* (April 1937), and later met them in Paris with Edith Sitwell. He refers to them as "this American couple." Beaton thinks Stein knew "she was very ill"; the photos taken during this time are "the most poignant."

17. ———. *The Wandering Years: Diaries: 1922-1939*. London: Weidenfeld and Nicolson, 1961.

   Beaton's diaries contain some information on Stein and Alice B. Toklas in the Rue Christine apartment and in Belley. He has a very artistic feeling for the set-up of the houses—where nothing was extraneous, and everything was well-ordered and highly polished—about which he writes very precisely. His feeling for Stein the personage does not seem to extend to Stein the writer; Beaton refers to one of her pieces as "rubbish."

18. Bell, Clive. *Old Friends: Personal Recollections*. London: Chatto and Windus, 1956.

   Bell's "recollections" contain two chapters on Paris. He did not think either Gertrude or Leo had an eye for "visual art."

   Among othe errors, "Stein" is alphabetized after "Stephens."

19. Blunt, Anthony and Phoebe Pool. *Picasso: The Formative Years: A Study of His Sources*. London: Studio Books, 1962.

    Although this study contains an entire section entitled "Guillaume Apollinaire and Gertrude Stein" (pp. 22-25), there are really only two paragraphs and a few other mentions concerned with Stein.

20. Brown, Frederick. *An Impersonation of Angels: A Biography of Jean Cocteau*. London: Longmans, 1968.

    Cocteau admitted to being inspired by Gertrude Stein. Brown says "Gertrude Stein could never quite bring herself to dislike Cocteau" because of this.

21. Burbank, Rex. *Thornton Wilder*. New York: Twayne, 1961.

    Chapter 4, Sec. 1 (pp. 81-87), "Gertrude Stein and Wilder's Literary Theories," concerns Stein's influence on Wilder.

22. Calas, Nicholas. *Confound the Wise*. New York: Arrow Editions, 1942.

23. Callaghan, Morley. *That Summer in Paris: Memories of Tangled Friendships with Hemingway, Fitzgerald, and Some Others*. New York: Coward-McCann, 1963.

    Mr. Callaghan's title reveals completely the contents of his book. He had no interest in meeting Stein, *Three Lives* was her only book, and "abstract prose was nonsense."

24. Cocteau, Jean. *My Contemporaries*. Ed. Margaret Crosland. London: Peter Owen, 1967.

25. ———. *Professional Secrets: An Autobiography*. Ed. Robert Phelps. New York: Farrar, Straus and Giroux, 1970.

26. Crespelle, Jean-Paul. *Picasso: Les Femmes, les amis, l'oeuvre*. Paris: Presse de la Cité, 1967.

27. ———. *Picasso and His Women*. Trans. Robert Baldick. London: Hodder and Stoughton, 1969.

Crespelle says the Steins were "vegetarians and adherents of Raymond Duncan's Naturist theories" around 1905-08. The short biography of Leo and Gertrude (pp. 104-05) contains inaccuracies and, mostly, misleading statements. Gertrude was an "insensitive blue-stocking."

Crespelle's book contains rather startlingly barbed passages, considering he knew neither Stein nor Alice B. Toklas; he is probably basing his statements on other memoirs of the period.

28. Crosby, Caresse. *The Passionate Years*. London: Alvin Kedman, 1955.

Harry Crosby's wife, née Polly Jacob, includes in her memoirs two pages treating of four different meetings with Stein over more than 10 years.

29. cummings, e.e. *Selected Letters of E. E. Cummings*. Ed. F. W. Dupee and George Stade. New York: Harcourt, 1969.

There are several references to Gertrude Stein, and to *Tender Buttons, Making of Americans, Wars I Have Seen,* and to some other 1940s books. Stein, at least, supported Henri Pétain.

30. Dijkstra, Bram. *The Hieroglyphics of a New Speech: Cubism, Stieglitz, and the Early Poetry of William Carlos Williams*. Princeton: Princeton University Press, 1969.

Dijkstra recounts Alfred Stieglitz's early "sponsorship of Gertrude Stein." He quotes Stieglitz's introduction to the special issue of *Camera Work*; Stieglitz wrote that Stein's portraits "and not the subjects with which they deal or the illustrations that accompany them, are the *raison d'etre* of this special issue."

31. Draper, Muriel. *Music at Midnight*. New York: Harper, 1929.

Draper's reminiscences are good to read to get an idea of life from 1909-14. They include a description of Gertrude and Alice, an incident concerning Stein's writing, an attempt to copy Stein's writing, and a photo from 1928. Draper also includes stories about Mabel Dodge, Henry James, and other important figures.

32. Dumas, Bethany K. *E. E. Cummings: A Remembrance of Miracles*. London: Vision, 1974.

Dumas refers to and quotes cummings's oft-referred to "The New Art" (1915) in which he speaks about Stein and reads from *Tender Buttons*. Stein's words "were the result of carrying the logic of literary sound painting to its extreme. Convinced that the results were indeed logical, [cummings] was not prepared to admit they were art."

33. Duncan, Isadora. *My Life*. London: Gollancz, 1928.

34. Fabre, Michel. *The Unfinished Quest of Richard Wright*. Trans. Isabel Barzun. New York: Morrow, 1973.

Fabre acknowledges Stein's influence on Wright's writing, and her help with his expatriation. He quotes Wright's articles on Stein. See *Black Boy: A Record of Childhood and Youth* (New York: Harper, 1945); "Gertrude Stein's Story Is Drenched in Hitler's Horrors" (*P.M. Magazine*, 11 March 1945, p.m. 15) for a review of *Wars I Have Seen* and Wright's famous comment on "Melanctha"; and "American G.I.'s Fears Worry Gertrude Stein" (*P.M. Magazine*, 26 July 1946, p.m. 15-16) for *Brewsie and Willie*.

35. Feibleman, James K. *The Way of a Man: An Autobiography*. New York: Horizon Press, 1969.

Feibleman describes briefly a dinner with Stein in New Orleans at the Roark Bradfords.

36. Fletcher, John Gould. *Life Is My Song: The
    Autobiography of John Gould Fletcher.* New York:
    Farrer and Rinehart, 1937.
    > Fletcher met Stein in 1913, and "was not ready . . . to
    > accord to her the epithet of 'genius'." He refers to her as
    > "ex-American Gertrude Stein."
    > Fletcher was mostly in London 1909-13.

37. Ford, Hugh. *Published in Paris: American and British
    Writers, Printers, and Publishers in Paris, 1920-1939.* New
    York: Macmillan, 1975.
    > See especially Chapter 6, "Gertrude Stein's Plain Editions"
    > (pp. 231-52). Janet Flanner wrote the intoduction, "A
    > Foreword: Three Amateur Publishers." Page 56ff. concerns Contact
    > Publishing and *The Making of Americans.* Ford also includes the
    > history of Stein's publishing elsewhere—in little presses, little
    > magazines, and Plain Edition—until Bennett Cerf.
    > "George Wilcox revealed that Miss Toklas once told him that
    > at Gertrude's insistence she had started to write a book of
    > memoirs to be called 'My 25 Years with Gertrude Stein', but
    > had found the writing so troublesome that she had accepted
    > Gertrude's help in making revisions and later allowed Gertrude
    > to take down her words and revise them as she went along.
    > As far as Miss Toklas was concerned, the *Autobiography* had always
    > been Gertrude's book."

38. Gillespie, A. Lincoln, Jr., et al. *Readies for Bob Brown's
    Machine.* Cagnes-sur-Mer (A.-M.): Roving Eye Press,
    1931.
    > *Readies* contains a piece by Gertrude Stein, "We Came a
    > History." In the appendix appears Bob Brown's *Readies.* Brown
    > did not know what Stein was up to in *Tender Buttons* but, in
    > 1914, "it was a case of champagne to me. . . . Gertrude
    > Stein gave me a great kick. . . . I began to see that a story might be
    > anything."

39. Gilot, Françoise and Carlton Lake. *Life with Picasso.*
New York: McGraw-Hill, 1965.

Between pp. 60 and 64 appears the story of Françoise's
first and only meeting with Alice and Gertrude, in the winter of
1944 (?) in the Rue Christine. Gertrude did not speak "very
good French." Alice's "accent . . . sounded like a music-
hall caricature of an American tourist reading from a French
phrase book." Gilot presents an ugly picture of Toklas (she
was frightened by Alice), but Gilot admired Stein; although
she only met the two once, she writes that she sometimes saw
Stein marketing alone.

40. Glasgow, Ellen. *Letters of Ellen Glasgow.* Comp. and
ed. Blair Rouse. New York: Harcourt, Brace,1958.

Letters contains one letter to Carl Van Vechten and one to
Mr. Alfred Harcourt in which Glasgow mentions Stein. In
February 1935, Stein and Toklas dined with Glasgow in Richmond.
Before the dinner, she wrote Van Vechten "I have
nothing against Gertrude Stein except what is popularly
known as her 'Influence'. My private opinion is that the writers
she has influenced . . . couldn't have been much worse if
she had let them alone." After the dinner, however, she wrote
that, due to Stein's personality, "we became very good
friends."

41. Glassco, John. *Memoirs of Montparnasse.* New York:
Oxford University Press, 1970.

Leon Edel describes Glassco's retelling of the one time he
visited Stein's salon as a "vignette." According to Edel, the
"essence" of Montparnasse before the war (about 1928-1932)
is in this book.

42. Goldstein, Malcolm. *The Art of Thornton Wilder.*
Lincoln: University of Nebraska Press, 1965.

The information on the Wilder-Stein relationship stems
from earlier books on Stein: John Malcolm Brinnin's *Third
Rose* (I-B-i-2), *Flowers of Friendship* (I-B-i-5), and *Everybody's
Autobiography.*
Wilder did not meet Stein on his 1920s trips to Europe. *Our*

Town was influenced by *Geographical History of America* and by Stein's lectures.

43. Grace, Harvey. *Musician at Large.* London: Oxford University Press, 1928.

44. Guggenheim, Peggy, ed. *Art of This Century. Objects, Drawings, Photographs, Sculpture, Collages 1910 to 1942.* New York: Art of This Century, 1942.

45. Guggenheim, Peggy. *Out of This Century: The Informal Memoirs of Peggy Guggenheim.* New York: Dial, 1946.

46. ———. *Confessions of an Art Addict.* New York: Macmillan, 1960.

47. Haberman, Donald. *The Plays of Thornton Wilder: A Critical Study.* Middletown, Connecticut: Wesleyan University Press, 1967.

   The section on Stein is mostly concerned with her idea of narration and her influence on Wilder. "A new definition of beauty emerged for Wilder from Gertrude Stein's theorizing about plays" in *Lectures in America.*

48. Hahn, Emily. *Romantic Rebels: An Informal History of Bohemianism in America.* Boston: Houghton Mifflin, 1967.

   Stein is discussed mainly between pp. 160 and 166. She was not a Bohemian, but "her contribution to America's Bohemia and the movement toward new art was enormous." The section on Stein is biographically unsound and insignificant.

49. Hall, Radclyffe. *The Well of Loneliness.* London: Jonathan Cape, 1928.

   Hall's novel provides an insight into the lesbian scene in Europe around the First World War and the prevailing psychological background of early twentieth-century lesbian novels.

50. Hamnett, Nina. *Laughing Torso: Reminiscences.*
    London: Constable, 1932.

   Hamnett was an artist who was in and out of Paris
   (Montparnasse) in the 1910s and 1920s. She knew most of the
   people Stein refers to in her work, and met Stein circa 1914
   (Hamnett saw Stein's art collection around this time).
   Hamnett and Stein were together at the Fords one Christmas;
   Hamnett writes of Stein's swinging her sandal on her big
   toe and of an encounter with Raymond Duncan.

51. Hapgood, Hutchins. *A Victorian in the Modern World.*
    New York: Harcourt, 1939.

   Hapgood writes of life on the continent before 1910 until
   1938. He had introduced the Steins to Bernard Berenson, and
   includes in his reminiscences a good "vignette" of Leo.
   "I felt in Gertrude Stein something wholly intense, not the sort of
   mental intensity I had seen in Bertrand Russell, whose
   activity seemed to me to consist of quick-coming and complex
   thoughts, tumultuous, one turning upon the other; but a deep
   temperamental life-quality, which was also inspiring." "The
   ego was apparent."

   Hapgood mentions a visit by Stein in Italy. He also mentions
   Three Lives and *The Autobiography of Alice B. Toklas*, and quotes
   from a *Globe* article written by him in which he makes "the
   comparison between the spiritual dynamites of those days
   and the impressionism" of Stein and Anton Johannsen. He
   quotes two other articles, written between 1911 and 1913,
   neither of which is very insightful but nevertheless are early
   considerations of Stein.

   Stein treated Ernest Hemingway badly in *Autobiography*,
   Hapgood writes, because Stein "is a particularly Jewish
   woman, in the sense that she feels her race intensely," and
   Hemingway had written disparagingly about Cohn in *The
   Sun Also Rises*.

52. Hemingway, Ernest. *The Green Hills of Africa*. New York: Scribner's, 1935.

"It's a damned shame, though, with all that talent gone to malice and nonsense and self-praise. . . . She never could write dialogue. . . . She learned how to do it from my stuff. . . ."

53. Hoover, Kathleen and John Cage. *Virgil Thomson: His Life and Music*. New York: Thomas Yoseloff, 1959.

Hoover writes much about the association/collaboration between Stein and Thomson, who met in 1926. The book contains, of course, the stories of *Four Saints in Three Acts* and *Mother of Us All*.

Four Saints

is dominated by the landscape of Avila . . . and like Avila it abounds in contrasts. . . . it induces a mood. . . . Neither saint, nor any of their apprentices, has dimension, yet all have immediacy. They are talkative abstractions rather than characters, but their patter generates an intellectual excitement as continuous as crisis in melodrama. In this sense *Four Saints* touches the dynamics of the Spanish theater, based on sustained verbal excitement rather than progress of action. Its failure to emulate the brevity of native Spanish opera could be considered its only shortcoming: ambiguous art is a potent drug best assimilated in discreet doses.

Stein had expected Thomson to cut or edit the libretto, but "he found the words so singable that he condensed it little. He even added characters, though no words."

"The fantasy [Stein] based on the battle for women's rights [*Mother of Us All*] blends historical and topical figures with her usual disdain for chronology, but the figures express themselves lucidly and with vehemence. . . . The dialogue is a reflection of personality rather than a vehicle for advancing a plot. . . .

". . . the musical setting of *The Mother of Us All* marks an advance in range of characterization. The intoned sermon, the political rallying song, the sentimental ballad, the parlor solo

on the piano, the Gospel tune in Salvation Army style,
together with original tunes with a nineteenth-century
American flavor, are all put to psychological uses. . . ."

"For the . . . devout episodes" of *Four Saints*, Thomson's
"music has the grave beauty of Anglican chant, but the brass
choir of American revivalist meetings and echoes of the
harmonium of rural American chapels pervade his
instrumentation. Where there are secular implications,
the parlor piece, the Stephen Foster ballads, and the dance
tunes of nineteenth-century America are evoked. Gertrude
Stein's esoteric fantasy emerged from Thomson's hands clad
in homespun. Yet his setting is anything but monotonously
local. It has Spanish overtones, madrigalian echoes of
Elizabethan England, and a Satiean humor resulting from
the deliberate discrepancy between text and score."

Hoover also gives some reasons for the success of *Four Saints
in Three Acts*.

John Cage lists all the music written by Thomson. Included
in the list are five pieces with words by Stein and two operas.
Also included is the Piano Sonata No. 3 (1930), humorously
written by Thomson for Stein.

54. Houseman, John. *Run-Through: A Memoir*. New York:
Simon and Schuster, 1972.

See Chapter 2, "The Apprentice Years (1931-1933); *Four
Saints in Three Acts* (1934)," for Houseman's history of *Four
Saints*. He describes the parts played in the production by
himself, Florine Stettheimer, Virgil Thomson, Kate Drain
Lawson, Frederick Ashton and Alexander Smallens.

55. Huddleston, Sisley. *Paris Salons, Cafes, Studios: Being
Social, Artistic and Literary Memoirs*. New York: Blue
Ribbon Books, 1928.

56. Imbs, Bravig. *Confessions of Another Young Man*. New York:
Henkle-Yewdale House, 1936.

Section 1 is on George Antheil, "The Sweet and Violent
George Antheil," and Section 2 is "In Love with Genius:
Gertrude Stein." Imbs's reminiscences cover Paris of the
1920s and 30s.

His book contains some errors, for instance the remark that

Stein "so liked it [Picasso's *Girl with a Basket of Flowers*] that she bought it for a hundred gold francs."

This is a chatty book, a who-was-who in Paris, filled with the gossip of the time. Imbs states that "Gertrude was a great success in French society whenever she appeared." Imbs's story concludes with his version of the hatcheting of Imbs, Virgil Thomson, Georges Hugnet et al.: Alice's fault.

57. Josephson, Matthew. *Life among the Surrealists: A Memoir.* New York: Holt, Rinehart and Winston, 1962.

These are the reminiscences of the 1920s which include a different rendition of the birth of the "Lost Generation" label, in addition to that accorded the auto mechanic. In the introduction to his book, Josephson deals rather lengthily with the question of expatriation.

He mentions hearing that e.e. cummings read a paper on Stein and Cubism at Harvard in 1915.

Josephson saw Stein as a " 'philosophical poet', with an extraordinary eye that saw all around things, and had a rare sense of humor as well."

58. Kahnweiler, Daniel-Henry. *Juan Gris: His Life and Work.* Trans. Douglas Cooper. London: Lund Humphries, 1947.

These are Kahnweiler's recollections of Gris's life, supported by excerpts from Gris's letters to Kahnweiler. It includes mentions of Stein.

"In the case of Gertrude Stein this [Cubist] spirit seems so intense and rigid that sometimes one has the false impression that she has reached the point of abstraction. She makes use of existing words without inventing any, but she uses the raw material of language with absolute liberty dictated by the logic of her work (if I may so describe her imperturbable flow, which does not unfold logically) and not in accordance with pre-existing laws." Stein "reduced" syntax "to its simplest form" but did preserve it.

59. Knoll, Robert E. *Robert McAlmon: Expatriate Publisher and Writer*. University of Nebraska Studies: New Series No. 18. Lincoln: University of Nebraska Press, August 1957.

> This pamphlet contains a long section on McAlmon as publisher, with some mentions of Stein.

60. Koch, Vivienne. *William Carlos Williams*. 1950; rpt. New York: Kraus Reprint, 1973.

> Stein is listed as one of the "three sources for the predominant narrative style" in *Knife of the Times*. Koch finds Stein's prose "cadenced, clear, syntactically functional."
>
> There are innumerable references to Stein in William Carlos Williams criticism.

61. Levy, Harriet. Memoirs of San Francisco. Unpublished, untitled, undated, ca. 1950. Bancroft Library.

> See also *920 O'Farrell Street* (New York: Doubleday, 1947).

62. Lewis, R.W.B. *Edith Wharton: A Biography*. New York: Harper and Row, 1976.

> Wharton lived in France during the same period as Stein and Alice B. Toklas; Lewis presents a Paris different from the one that we meet through Stein.

63. Longstreet, Stephen. *We All Went to Paris: Americans in the City of Light: 1776-1971*. New York: Macmillan, 1972.

> See Chapter 27, "La Stein"; 28, "Gertrude in Glory"; 47, "Lost Days of Gertrude and Alice"; 48, "Americans with Music—Harris, Thomson, etc." "Much that has been written [about Stein's Paris] is hasty journalism or pedantic autopsis by the university presses. A great deal of the material is made of myth and legend. Survivors have added their faulty memories to take part in the action; much of their histories is suspect. . . ." Longstreet refers to Stein's brother "Willy," ignores her sister, and claims "Their growing up was done in

San Francisco." Leo Stein's book is *"Journey into Myself."* His chronology is confused; he implies that *What Is Remembered* appeared before the *Alice B. Toklas Cookbook,* whose author died in 1966. There is no index.

See also the sections "Hemingway," "At Natalie Barney's," and so on. See George Wickes, I-B-ii-97.

64. Lueders, Edward. *Carl Van Vechten.* New York: Twayne, 1965.

Van Vechten met Stein and Alice B. Toklas in 1913.

Lueders, on an entry in Van Vechten's autograph book, writes the following: "An entry for August 6, 1930, in Paris is, like much of what Miss Stein wrote, a miniature, as closed and polished as a heroic couplet by Pope, yet as open and spontaneous as the utterance of a precocious child. It may be at once the most ingenious and ingenuous epigraph to a literary relationship written in our time. In any event, it is an index to their friendship and a prime example of the affirmative existentialism they both exemplified:

August 6, 1930

'Carl is here which is a pleasure we are here which is a pleasure, and we all like nougat.

Gtde Stein'."

Lueders writes with some bias about Van Vechten's guidance and companionship. He mentions *Autobiography of Alice B. Toklas* as "a delightfully transparent use of the technique" (of autobiography as biography?).

In *Nigger Heaven,* Van Vechten's Mary Love quotes passages from "Melanctha" by heart.

65. Luhan, Mabel Dodge. *Intimate Memories.* 4 vols. Vol. 2: *European Experiences.* New York: Harcourt, 1935. Vol. 3: *Movers and Shakers.* New York: Harcourt, 1936.

This is, of course, the autobiography of a woman born about the same time as Stein and Alice B. Toklas, a woman who was well traveled and certainly knew a great number of the "leading figures" of the time.

Intimate Memories fills in much about the style and feeling of life in Europe and acts as an introduction to Gertrude and Alice in Europe. In its own right, this autobiography is very interesting; as far as it concerns Alice and Gertrude, most of the information has been reprinted or retold in later books.

Volumes 2 and 3 provide information on Stein and Toklas. Villa Curonia episodes are related in Vol. 2, Chapter 13, "The Steins." Alice provided "the motor force of the menage. . . . And Gertrude was growing helpless and foolish from it and less and less inclined to do anything herself, Leo said. . . ." This chapter also contains the story of Gertrude's writing of "Mabel Dodge at the Villa Curonia," as well as lengthy quotations from it. Mabel Dodge also gives her own version of her break with Stein.

Vol. 3 contains a chapter on Leo (Chapter 12), and reprints 10 letters from Gertrude Stein (pp. 29-36). Also included are portions of Mabel Dodge's "Speculations, or Post Impressions in Prose," which appeared in *Arts and Decorations*, 3 (1913), 172-74. "She [Stein] is impelling language to induce new states of consciousness, and in doing so language becomes with her a creative art rather than a mirror of history." See Vol. 3 for Dodge's article and her theory of Stein's working habits.

66. McAlmon, Robert. *Being Geniuses Together*. London: Secker and Warburg, 1938.

Chapter 11, "Genius All too Simple," deals exclusively with Stein and the Contact Editions' *Making of Americans* fiasco.

67. ———. *McAlmon and the Lost Generation: A Self-Portrait*. Ed. Robert E. Knoll. Lincoln: University of Nebraska Press, 1962.

A memoir of the founder of Contact Editions, a writer and publisher, this contains a great deal of material from *Being Geniuses Together* (at least from the first three sections). It contains the information that five copies of *Making of Americans* were "refused entry at New York" due to suspicions of anything "printed in English on the continent"; 100 copies had already been sold in America.

See especially "Genius All too Simple," pp. 199-207, which contains a more objective version by Knoll of the *Making of Americans* problems. Also included is part of the *Outlook* review

of *Making of Americans*. Reprinted is the "Portrait" of Stein
which originally appeared in Pound's *Exile*.

68. **Man Ray.** *Self Portrait*. **London: Andre Deutsch,
1963.**

   When Man Ray first met Stein, her hair was "cropped after
an illness." He visited Stein off and on for 10 years.

69. **Marks, Barry A.** *E. E. Cummings*. **New York: Twayne,
1964.**

   "The New Art" is quoted.

70. **Norman, Charles.** *E. E. Cummings: The Magic Maker*.
New York: Bobbs-Merrill, 1972.

   Norman quotes a large section from cummings's "The New
Art." " 'Gertrude Stein is a Futurist who subordinates the
meaning of words to the beauty of the words themselves. Her
art is the logic of literary sound-painting carried to its
extreme. While we must admit that it is logic, must we admit that
it is Art?' "

71. **Olivier, Fernande (Fernande Belvallée).** *Picasso et
ses Amis*. **Paris: Librairie Stock, Delamain et
Boutelleau, 1933.**

   See following entry. (Interestingly enough, this follows the
publication of *Autobiography of Alice B. Toklas*.)

72. ———. *Picasso and His Friends*. **Trans. Jane Miller.
London: Heinemann, 1964.**

   "Art Lovers and Collectors" contains either factual errors or
miscomprehensions. "Saturday at the Steins" covers 1910-1914
and contains the story of the Steins varnishing two Picassos.
   Olivier writes about Paris, 1903-1914; she offers a good
background book, albeit with the natural bias of Picasso's
mistress. The Montparnasse group broke up, she says, when
everyone began making money.

73. Pollack, Barbara. *The Collectors: Dr. Claribel and Miss Etta Cone with a "Portrait" by Gertrude Stein*. New York: Bobbs-Merrill, 1962.

Pollack describes briefly the life of German-Jewish immigrants. This provides a very good background; the Cones knew Leo and Gertrude in Baltimore, and Pollack gives a more than adequately detailed account of these years and the early years in Europe. Included are letters from the Steins to Etta and Claribel. Pollack's is definitely a biography of the Cones, whose lives were very entwined with the Steins.

74. Putnam, Samuel. *Paris Was Our Mistress*. New York: Viking, 1947.

Chapter 5, "From a Latin Quarter Sketchbook," part 3, "The Woman with a Face Like Caesar's," is a spoof; it appears to be an interview drawn from abstruse quotations in books.

There are many more mentions of Stein. "Hemingway, I reflected, *had* learned something from Stein: something about what Stein calls 'the rhythm of the visible universe'." Putnam was afraid of Stein; she reminded him of Amy Lowell. Putnam thinks *transition* "performed an invaluable service" by publishing James Joyce and Stein.

He touches on the Jolas-Stein quarrel and speaks of "the chronic petulance of the long-term expatriate (a Pound or a Stein)."

75. Rose, Francis. *Saying Life: The Memoirs of Sir Francis Rose*. London: Cassell, 1961.

Rose's autobiography should dispel any past malignancy about Stein's egocentricity.

Saying Life is dedicated "TO a great mind who helped to build the twentieth century [,] GERTRUDE STEIN [,] writer and inventor of the new American language; a poet and playwright and art collector with a clear and precise mind"; and contains a complete chapter on Stein. It tends to be interesting not because of the author but because it is the

story of a mediocre artist sponsored by Stein in her later years
and contains his impressions of her. Again, the errors, factual
and spelling, are multitudinous. Rose refers to Florine
Stettheimer as "Stadthimer" and "Stadtheimer" and to
Kristians Tonny as "Toni" and "Tony."

"It had always been Gertrude Stein's intention to write a
detective story called *Blood on the Dining-room Floor*, but death
cheated her from ever achieving this game of words." (*Blood
on the Dining Room Floor* was written in 1933.)

Toklas was "descended from a line of great Polish Rabbis"
(this cannot be substantiated by any other literature), and
Stein was Episcopalian and "a practicing Christian" (false).

"Before I left, [Hermann Goering] promised that should
anything happen to France, he would see that Gertrude Stein
and Alice Toklas would be safe and never be in financial
need."

76. Rosenshine, Annette. "Life's Not a Paragraph."
Bancroft Library, University of California, Berkeley.

Annette Rosenshine was related to Alice B. Toklas, first
met her around 1886, and kept up a correspondence with her
until Toklas's death.

77. Schneps, Maurice. *Woman at St. Lô*. Tokyo: Cross
Continent, 1959.

"Gertrude Stein: A Brief Encounter" concerns an attempt
at philosophical conversation with Stein in 1944. It is based
on notes taken 15 years before the writing of this chapter.

Stein was "a powerful personality, of brilliant mind, but . . .
of rather narrow perspectives." Schneps includes a few words
of criticism on *Three Lives, Narration, Lectures in America,
Autobiography of Alice B. Toklas,* and *Brewsie and Willie.*

78. Secrest, Meryle. *Between Me and Life: A Biography of
Romaine Brooks.* New York: Doubleday, 1974.

Romaine Brooks, an American artist, was an expatriate in
Paris at the same time as Gertrude and Alice. She was also
Natalie Barney's lover and a sometimes frequenter of Barney's
salon. Both *Between Me and Life* and Radclyffe Hall's *Well of*

Loneliness (I-B-ii-49) contribute an insight into the consciousness
of the early-twentieth-century lesbian and into the
homosexual scene in Paris.

79. Seroff, Victor. *The Real Isadora*. London:
    Hutchinson, 1972.

Seroff's biography contains no information on Stein, but parts of
it will add to an understanding of the American
expatriate in Paris.

80. Sevareid, Eric. *Not So Wild a Dream*. New York:
    Knopf, 1946.

Sevareid first met Stein in late 1937 or 1938, and was very
impressed by her. Stein had just finished *"Faust"* (sic), which
she read in part to Sevareid, who published it. (Perhaps
Sevareid is referring to *Dr. Faustus Lights the Lights*; if so, he
did not publish it; *Dr. Faustus* was first published in *Last Operas and
Plays*. I am unable to trace Sevareid's reference further. If this
is a 1938 play—and if Sevareid has forgotten not only the title
but also the subject of the play—it might be *Lucretia Borgia*,
published in *Creative Writing* in 1938; or, more likely, a 1937
sketch called "Ida" [published in 1938 in *Boudoir Companion*]
[Robert Bartlett Haas refers, in *How Writing Is Written*, to "Ida"
as a "short novella"], referred to by Stein as "an opera about
Faust" [letter to Thornton Wilder, quoted by Richard
Bridgman (II-A-2) in *Gertrude Stein in Pieces*].)

"She has a remarkably lucid and germinal mind and
disguises a profound understanding by a simplicity of
rapidly flowing speech that misleads the casual listener. A
conditioned mind like mine, trained to the conventional
formulae of expression, could retain her ideas clearly but
was quite unable, later, to reproduce her own words. They were
too basic, too simple. In written form her words seem bizarre
and difficult to follow, but when she herself reads them
aloud it is all perfectly lucid, natural, and exact."

The major section on Stein concerns her "liberation."
Sevareid refers to Stein, "whose works were on Goebbels'
blacklist" (compare with Francis Rose's statement in *Saying
Life*, I-B-ii-75). Sevareid also writes about Stein in Culoz

immediately after her liberation and includes a shorter version of her famous broadcast from Voiron.

81. Shattuck, Roger. *The Banquet Years: The Arts in France 1885-1918*. London: Faber and Faber, 1959.

   Shattuck sees a similarity between Jean-Paul Sartre's description of Albert Camus's style and Donald Sutherland's (II-A-16) of Stein's. There are some mentions of Stein and some quotations.

82. ———. *The Banquet Years: The Origin of the Avant-Garde in France: 1885 to World War I*. Rev. ed. London: Jonathan Cape, 1969.

   See preceding entry.

83. Slocombe, George. *The Tumult and the Shouting: The Memoirs of George Slocombe*. London: Heinemann, 1936.

   Slocombe met Stein once, when she was modelling for the Jo Davidson sculpture.

84. Sprigge, Elizabeth and Jean-Jacques Kihm. *Jean Cocteau: The Man and the Mirror*. London: Gollancz, 1968.

   There are only two mentions of Stein, but this book provides useful background information: it is the biography of someone who knew Stein and most of the same people she knew, who lived in Paris, who was also an artist, and so on.

85. Squires, Radcliffe. *Allen Tate: A Literary Biography*. New York: Pegasus, 1971.

   Quoting liberally from Tate's (?) "Random Thoughts on the Twenties" (*Minnesota Review*, 1 [Fall 1960] 53), and from a 1929 letter to Mark Van Doren, Squires recounts Tate's meeting with Stein.

86. Stein, Amelia Keyser. "Diary." 5 Volumes, from January 1878 to September 1886, not continuous. Bancroft Library, University of California, Berkeley.

> See references to Amelia Stein's diary in the biographies and in Richard Bridgman (II-A-2). Gertrude Stein's mother died in 1888, so the diaries give a somewhat sporadic account of the family until Gertrude's twelfth year.

87. Stein, Leo. *Appreciation: Painting, Poetry and Prose.* New York: Crown Publishers, 1947.

88. ———. *Journey into the Self: Being the Letters, Papers, and Journals of Leo Stein,* Ed. Edmund Fuller. New York: Crown, 1950.

> *Journey into the Self* and *Appreciation* (preceding entry) provide Leo Stein's opinions on Gertrude and her writing, her style of life, her art collection, and so forth.

89. Stephens, Robert O. *Hemingway's Nonfiction: The Public Voice.* Chapel Hill: University of North Carolina Press, 1968.

> Perhaps the most interesting section for Stein research is that concerning Stein and Ernest Hemingway's "feud"; this reconstruction is based on Hemingway's nonfiction writings and on sections of *The Sun Also Rises* and *Torrents of Spring.*

90. Stevens, Wallace. *Letters of Wallace Stevens.* Sel. and ed. Holly Stevens. New York: Knopf, 1966.

> In a 1934 letter to Harriet Monroe, Stevens writes that *Four Saints in Three Acts* "is an elaborate bit of perversity in every respect: text, settings, choreography, it is most agreeable musically, so that, if one excludes aesthetic self-consciousness from one's attitude, the opera immediately becomes a delicate and joyous work all round."

91. Thomson, Virgil. *Virgil Thomson.* New York: Knopf, 1966.

> This is Thomson's light, easy-to-read, factual autobiography,

in his inimitably egotistical style. His friendship with Stein
and Alice B. Toklas dates from 1925-26, and there is much
about them in his autobiography. He refers to "my opera . . .
for which Gertrude Stein had written the libretto." Chapter
9, "Langlois, Butts, and Stein," contains a great deal of
information on Stein and Toklas. Thomson puts forward the
theory behind his first setting Stein's words to music, and
his explanation of the finding of the theme for *Four Saints in
Three Acts*.

Thomson brought about the "eventual performance and
musical publication of these works" (pieces by Stein, music
by Thomson). Included is a large section on the composition
of *Four Saints in Three Acts* and a defense against the negative
musical criticism of his opera.

"The literary consensus is always that the music is lovely
but the poetry absurd; whereas the music world, at least nine
tenths of it, takes the view that Stein's words are great
literature but that my music is infantile."

Chapter 15 is entitled "A Portrait of Gertrude Stein" and
Chapter 16 "Gertrude and the Young French Poet." In these
chapters Thomson delves into literary criticism. Stein
developed a "new literary style" in "Ada" "by imitating Alice
Toklas" and then did not use it again for 23 years
(in *Autobiography of Alice B. Toklas*; see Richard Bridgman,
Gertrude Stein in Pieces [II-A-2], on the composition of
Autobiography). Stein's work exhibits constant growth.

The most interesting portions of this book for Stein
students are the sections concerning *Four Saints in Three Acts*.

92. Unterecker, John. *Voyager: A Life of Hart Crane*. New
York: Farrar, Straus and Giroux, 1969.

93. Van Vechten, Carl. *Fragments from an Unwritten
Autobiography*. 2 vols. New Haven: Yale University
Press, 1955.

In Volume 2 appears "Some 'Literary Ladies' I Have
Known," of which a portion is reminiscence about Stein and
Alice B. Toklas.

94. Vollard, Ambroise. *Recollections of a Picture Dealer.*
Trans. Violet M. MacDonald. London: Constable,
1936.
> "The Steins and Other Americans" is Chapter 16. Vollard
> makes obvious errors about people and events.

95. ———. *Souvenirs d'un Marchand de Tableaux.* Paris: Éditions
Albin Michel, 1937.
> There are some differences in these two versions, e.g., some
> phrases in the English that are not in the French, words in the
> French not in the English. MacDonald, for instance, has "X's
> studio"; the original has "l'atelier de Matisse."

96. Webb, Constance. *Richard Wright: A Biography.* New
York: Putnam's Sons, 1968.
> Stein and "Melanctha" play a role in Wright's biography.
> Stein met Wright at Gare St. Lazare in 1946, and they "had
> long talks" in July.
> "This section on Gertrude Stein is based on notes made by
> the author during long conversations with Richard Wright
> after his return from France in 1947."

97. Wickes, George. *Americans in Paris.* New York:
Doubleday, 1969.
> See especially Section 1, "Gertrude Stein, the Mother of Us
> All," 1. "27 rue de Fleurus," 2. "Postimpressionism in Prose,"
> and 3. "The Autobiography of Gertrude Stein and Alice B.
> Toklas," pp. 15-64. Thomson and Stein are discussed, pp.
> 217–225+. Wickes mentions *Paris France, Three Lives, Making
> of Americans, Four Saints,* some of the portraits, *Tender Buttons,*
> and *Autobiography,* as well as works by Toklas. *Autobiography*
> and *Moveable Feast* are "ingeniously wrought fictions."
> "The *Autobiography* is highly inaccurate, with events revised
> to suit the author's convenience. Gertrude Stein treats facts
> with insouciance, ignoring those that do not interest her,
> modifying others, highlighting those she finds most dramatic
> or significant. In order to concentrate on a few main characters,
> she relegates the others to minor roles or suppresses them
> entirely. . . . Her   treatment   of   dates   is   particularly

carefree. . . . The legend was more poignant than the anticlimactic fact. Invariably she is more interested in telling a good story than telling the truth."

Wickes says parts of *Picasso et Ses Amis* (I-B-ii-71) appear in 1931. He compares it with *Autobiography*; Stein's versions are "often more convincing"; "more incisive, more characteristic, more vivid, more memorable." "The entire *Autobiography*. . . is controlled by a firm sense of purpose," which allows Stein to include as many anecdotes as possible.

98. ———. "Sketches of the Author's Life in Paris in the Twenties," in *Hemingway: In Our Time*. Eds. Richard Astro and Jackson J. Benson. Corvallis: Oregon State University Press, 1974. Pp. 25-38.

On Hemingway's many debts to Stein and on *A Moveable Feast*.

99. ———. *The Amazon of Letters: The Life and Loves of Natalie Barney*. New York: Putnam's, 1976.

Wickes includes several mentions of Stein and Alice B. Toklas, and presents a very interesting look at another Paris salon and its habituees.

100. Wolff, Geoffrey. *Black Sun: The Brief Transit and Violent Eclipse of Harry Crosby*. New York: Random House, 1976.

This is, of necessity, a selected listing. Autobiographies, biographies, and memoirs of anyone in Paris in the 1920s, or in Europe between 1900 and 1950, will provide background information, if not mentions of Stein. Obvious examples are Konrad Bercovici, Lord Berners, George Biddle, Maxwell Bodenheim, Fanny Butcher, Mary Butts, Emanuel Carnevali, Robert M. Coates, Marguerite D'Alvarez, Norman Douglas, Donald Friede, Ben Hecht, Alfred

Kreymbourg, Harold Loeb, Lady Diana Manners, Harriet Monroe, Grace Moore, Siegfried Sassoon, Pavel Tchelitchew, and Glenway Wescott. This list could be extended indefinitely.

iii.   Biographical and Memorial Articles

1. Hemingway, Ernest. "My Own Life." *New Yorker*, 2 (12 February 1927), 23.

    This article contains "The True Story of My Break with Gertrude Stein."

2. Faÿ, Bernard. "A Rose Is a Rose." *Saturday Review*, 10 (2 September 1933), 77-79.

    This is some type of reminiscent, stream-of-conscious monolog of an anecdotal nature around *Autobiography of Alice B. Toklas*.

3. Van Vechten, Carl. "On Words and Music." *New York Times*, 18 February 1934, Sec. 9, p. 2.

    In his letter of 13 February 1934—"in the Drama Editor's Mail"—Van Vechten writes of the "rather miraculous music drama," for which one needs "receptive passivity."

4. Warren, Lansing. "Gertrude Stein Views Life and Politics." *New York Times*, 6 May 1934, Sec. 6, p. 9.

5. Anon. "Gertrude Stein Arrives and Baffles Reporters by Making Herself Clear." *New York Times*, 25 October 1934, p. 25.

    This is an interview aboard *Champlain* on Stein's arrival in the United States. An editorial on her arrival, coupled with a short criticism of *Autobiography of Alice B. Toklas*, appears in *New York Times*, 25 October 1934, p. 20.

6. Anon. "Miss Stein Speaks to Bewildered 500." *New York Times*, 2 November 1934, p. 25.

   This news article covers Stein's lecture to Museum of Modern Art members on November 1. An editorial which is a brief spoof of this lecture appears in the *New York Times*, 3 November 1934, p. 14.

7. Anon. "Princeton Dazed by Gertrude Stein." *New York Times*, 6 November 1934, p. 23.

   Stein's Princeton visit is reported; some negative editorializing is included.

8. Anon. "Gertrude Stein and the Pigeon." *New York Times*, 8 November 1934, p. 22.

9. Anon. "Stein Likes Stein Opera." *New York Times*, 9 November 1934, p. 24.

10. Anon. "Quite Understandable." *Art Digest*, 9 (15 November 1934), 18 and 20.

    This is a news report of Stein's first lecture in America, to the members of the Museum of Modern Art.

11. Anon. "Miss Stein Uses Saints As Scenery." *New York Times*, 17 November 1934, p. 13.

    Another news article written while Stein was in America, this one reports on a musicale luncheon at the Ritz Hotel and on a contemporary literature class at Columbia.

12. Matthews, T. S. "Gertrude Stein Comes Home." *New Republic*, 81 (5 December 1934), 100–01.

    These are Matthews's impressions of Stein, gathered from a lecture given in the United States. This is reprinted in the *Essay Annual* (Chicago: Scott, Foresman) of 1935.

13. Anon. "Youth Understands Says Gertrude Stein."
    New York Times, 5 May 1935, p. 33.

    This article reports an interview with Stein before she
    returned to France; "Gertrude Stein Tells Paris She Is 'Wed
    to America' " (*New York Times*, 13 May 1935, p. 8) reports her
    return to France.

14. Preston, John Hyde. "Conversation." *Atlantic
    Monthly*, 156 (August 1935), 187-94.

    "Conversation" stems from a meeting with Stein in May
    1935 and presents her views on art and writing.

15. Levy, Harriet. "Neighbors." *Menorah Journal*, 25
    (April 1937), 187-90.

16. Ulrich, Dorothy Livingston. "Gertrude Stein in
    Summer." *Avocation*, 3 (February 1939), 309–15.

17. Bonney, Thérèse. "Gertrude Stein in France."
    Vogue, 100 (1 July 1942), 60-61, 70.

    Bonney records Stein's life in Billignen (sic) par Belley Ain
    after the fall of France. The article contains some interesting
    biographical notes, pictures, portions of Stein's letters, and
    Stein's comments on *Mrs. Reynolds*.

18. Cerf, Bennett. "Trade Winds." *Saturday Review*, 25
    (5 September 1942), 20.

    Cerf, Stein's publisher, devotes a complete column to
    anecdotes about her stay in America, his 1936 visit with
    her in Bilignin, her present occupations in unoccupied
    France.

19. Knauth, Percy. "War Is a War Is a War: Gertrude
    Stein Gives GIs a Lecture on Deportment." *Life*, 18
    (16 April 1945), 14 and 17-18.

20. Corbett, Scott. "Give Me Land." *Yank*, 2 (11
    November 1945), 17.

21. Anon. "Gertrude Stein Dies in France, 72." *New York Times*, 28 July 1946, p. 40.

     This obituary consists of two columns, and contains several errors.

22. Anon. Obituary of Gertrude Stein. *Nation*, 163 (10 August 1946), 142-43.

     "Legends never die, and Miss Stein had made herself into an American legend more lasting than anything Barnum himself ever created. . . ."

23. Genêt (Janet Flanner). "Letter from Paris." *New Yorker*, 22 (10 August 1946), 41-43.

     This is an obituary of Stein.

24. Smith, Harrison. "Rose for Remembrance." *Saturday Review*, 29 (10 August 1946), 11.

     This obituary remembers, paraphrases and condenses who and what Stein was and what and how her theories were. Smith sees Stein as very important to twentieth-century writing, and implicitly puts down the critics who had jeered so long, frequently using sentences much more complex and abstruse than Stein's.

25. Fremantle, Anne. "Mom in the Kitchen." *Commonweal*, 45 (25 October 1946), 33-34.

     Both this article and Fremantle's letter (*Commonweal*, 45 [20 December 1946], 253-54) contain many biographical errors. The letter is based on Jacques Maritain and on Stein's awareness that "the word is also the Word."

26. Rago, Henry. "Gertrude Stein." *Poetry*, 69 (November 1946), 93-97.

     Rago, an editor of *Poetry*, had met Stein in Paris (probably early 1945). His article is an obituary of sorts with some commentary on her theories.

27. Sorby, James Thrall. "Gertrude Stein and the Artists." *Saturday Review*, 30 (24 May 1947), 34-36.

28. Anon. "Lots of Fun." *New Yorker*, 23 (31 May 1947), 19-20.

This is a mention of "a collection of Gertrude Stein memorabilia on exhibition at the Yale Library."

29. Anon. "Speaking of Pictures: Gertrude Stein Left a Hodge-Podge behind Her." *Life*, 23 (18 August 1947), 14-16.

This brief article is concerned with the vast amounts of memorabilia shipped by Stein to the Yale University Library since 1938. Most interesting are the photographs reproduced, together with reproductions of letters Stein received and of a manuscript page of *Here*.

30. Clemens, Cyril. "A Chat with Gertrude Stein." *Hobbies*, 52 (October 1947), 145 and 150.

Stein had tea with Clemens in St. Louis. There are biographical errors in the article, which is a cross-section of quotations (from the lectures?) and spoof.

31. Porter, Katherine Anne. "Gertrude Stein: A Self Portrait." *Harper's Magazine*, 195 (December 1947), 519-28.

This was later published as "Wooden Umbrella," and is something between an obituary and a history of Stein, the Lost Generation, and so on. Porter hears overtones of sloth, boredom, avarice in Stein, whose mind was ". . . so long shapeless and undisciplined."

32. Herbst, Josephine. "Miss Porter and Miss Stein." *Partisan Review*, 15 (May 1948), 568-72.

Herbst compares Katherine Anne Porter's "Gertrude Stein" to Picasso's. Somehow she manages to use the comparison as a stepping stone into a monolog on modernism/communism/responsibility/individuality.

33. Gallup, Donald. "The Weaving of a Pattern: Marsden Hartley and Gertrude Stein." *Magazine of Art*, 41 (November 1948), 256-61.

   The correspondence of Marsden Hartley to Gertrude Stein, 1912-1934, is printed here. Gallup's commentary is more concerned with Hartley's search for self than with Stein's beneficence, although she is omnipresent in the article, through the letters.

34. Van Vechten, Carl. "Some 'Literary Ladies' I Have Known." *Yale University Library Gazette*, 26, No. 3 (January 1952), 97-116.

   See I-B-ii-93.

35. Duncan, Roland. Interview with Alice B. Toklas in Paris, 28-29 November 1952. Bancroft Library, University of California, Berkeley.

36. Anon. "Obliging Man." *Time*, 12 January 1953, p. 46.

   In this interview, Thornton Wilder states that everything "fell into place as he listened to [Gertrude Stein]."

37. Sprigge, Elizabeth. "Gertrude Stein's American Years." *Reporter*, 13 (11 August 1955), 46-52.

   Save for Sprigge's persistent use of the first-person singular as she pieces together bits of information and raises ghosts throughout her pilgrimage, this could have been an interesting reconstruction of the American Steins from 1841 through 1914. Some of the facts seem askew, but this might be due to the fact that the research was still in its early stages. She attempts here to capture the personality and psychology of Gertrude Stein.

38. Saarinen, Aline B. "Americans in Paris: Gertrude, Leo, Michael and Sarah Stein." *Proud Possessors: The Lives, Times and Tastes of Some Adventurous American Art Collectors.* New York: Random House, 1958. Pp. 174-205.

    This gives more background than the following article.

39. ———. "Stein in Paris." *American Scholar,* 27 (August 1958), 437-48.

40. Brinnin, John Malcolm. "Gertrude Stein in Paris." *Atlantic Monthly,* 204 (September 1959), 34-40.

41. ———. "Gertrude Stein in America." *Atlantic Monthly,* 204 (October 1959), 98-106.

42. Kahnweiler, Daniel-Henry. "Erinnerungen an Gertrude Stein." *Augenblick,* 5, No. 1 (1960), 1-10.

43. Yates, Peter. "Portrait of Gertrude Stein." *Forum* (Houston), 3, No. 4 (1960), 62-66.

44. Steele, Oliver L. "Gertrude Stein and Ellen Glasgow: Memoir of a Meeting." *American Literature,* 33 (March 1961), 76-77.

    This is a memoir, from one of Glasgow's notebooks, of a meeting between Glasgow and Stein, 5 February 1935.

45. Genêt (Janet Flanner). "Letter from Paris." *New Yorker,* 37 (16 December 1961), 106 and 108-09; 38 (29 December 1962), 66-68; 43 (25 March 1967), 174 and 177.

    Flanner's letters concern Alice B. Toklas after Gertrude Stein's death—Stein's will, Toklas's loss of the art collection, *What Is Remembered*—and include Toklas's obituary.

46. Chase, Mary Ellen. "Five Literary Portraits."
Massachusetts Review, 3 (Spring 1962), 511-16.

A remembrance of Stein on an afternoon in 1936
in Cambridge, England, appears on pp. 513-14.

47. Hemingway, Ernest. *A Moveable Feast*. New York:
Scribner's, 1964.

Hemingway's last attempts to give his side of the story
concerning Hemingway and Stein appear in "Miss Stein
Instructs," " 'Une Génération Perdue'," and "A Strange
Enough Ending." Although sections of these pieces are very
balanced and controlled, the malicious wins out.

48. Reeve, Gillian. "The Public I." *Manchester Guardian*,
9 November 1964, p. 8.

It happened 30 years ago today. The article is about
Stein's trip to the United States—why she went, what she did
there.

49. Shaw, Barnett. "Encounter with Gertrude Stein,
Paris, 1944." *Texas Quarterly*, 9, No. 3 (Autumn
1966), 21-23.

This is a reminiscence of Stein and Alice B. Toklas
immediately after their return to Paris at the end of the
German occupation.

50. Anon. "Alice Toklas, 89, Is Dead in Paris." *New York
Times*, 8 March 1967, p. 45.

An obituary, and an acclamation, of Alice B. Toklas, this
article also fills in a few facts about Stein's and Toklas's
lives; it also mentions that the last chapter of *What Is
Remembered* (see I-B-i-20) was not published, and that Toklas
left all her papers to Yale.

51. Barry, Joseph. "Alice B. Toklas." *Village Voice*, 16
March 1967, p. 8.

This is an obituary and a remembrance.

52. Harrison, Gilbert A. "Alice B. Toklas." *New Republic*, 156 (18 March 1967), 24 and 37.

This is a highly sympathetic memoir of Alice B. Toklas. Harrison dwells mostly on Toklas's life after 1946, but also includes some bits and pieces of her life with Stein. Harrison shows Alice as having a life and intellect and integrity of her own.

53. Anon. Obituary of Alice B. Toklas. *Publisher's Weekly*, 191 (20 March 1967), 42.

Contrary to the information contained in this article, Alice B. Toklas published neither cookbooks nor memoirs until after 1946.

54. Barry, Naomi. "Paris à table: A Memory of Alice B. Toklas." *Gourmet*, 27 (August 1967), 13, 28 and 30.

The article contains some biographical errors.

55. More de Morinni, Clara. "Miss Stein and the Ladies." *New Republic*, 157 (11 November 1967), 17-19.

This is the account of an unscheduled lecture Stein gave the American Women's Club in Paris, 8 December 1933.

56. Friedrich, Otto. "The Grave of Alice B. Toklas." *Esquire*, 69 (January 1968), 98-103 and 121-24.

The main problem with this article is the search "for the much newer grave that the newspapers said would be next to [Gertrude Stein's], the grave of Alice B. Toklas," which turns out to be "just an empty patch of dirt, slightly humped in the center, and there are two or three shards of broken pottery, and bits of glass, and a piece of brick, the kind of debris that always appears when the earth is dug up and then replaced." The only minor problem with this description is that it constitutes the sole reference that I have found to Alice's being buried in a separate grave in Père Lachaise. Gilbert A. Harrison, in his introduction to *Staying on Alone*, writes: "The plain coffin was driven one block to the parish church, then on through the thickest Paris traffic, winding about the Père

Lachaise Cemetery until the opened vault [sic] of Gertrude
Stein was reached. . . ." And W. G. Rogers, in *Gertrude Stein
Is Gertrude Stein* . . . (I-B-i-12), writes that "she was buried
beside Gertrude Stein" and that "the fine plain headstone is
the width of the two graves"; this could mean that Stein was
buried in a double plot (although it does not appear to be so
large), but it definitely does not mean that Toklas was buried
in the next grave. *Charmed Circle*, by James R. Mellow (I-B-i-9),
implies, by quoting Toklas's wish in her will that she be buried
"in the same tomb as Gertrude Stein in the Père Lachaise
Cemetery," that they have a common grave. In fact,
the newspaper article which leads Friedrich on his search states
that "Miss Toklas will be buried beside Miss
Stein. . . ."

"Like any twenty-year-old, I was interested mainly in
myself," says Friedrich, and "The Grave of Alice B. Toklas"
dwells much more on his attempts to become a successful
writer than on his visits with Toklas—who, it seems, was
practically his patron.

"*The Autobiography* is not a cute version of Gertrude Stein's
autobiography but literally the judgments, the views, the
language, the tone, and the quality of mind of Alice B. Toklas
herself. As such, as the re-creation of someone else's
personality, it is not only Miss Stein's best work but one of the
minor masterpieces of this century."

57. Hess, John L. "Sale of Stein Art Planned by Heirs."
New York Times, 31 January 1968, p. 38.

58. Glueck, Grace. "Gertrude Stein's Art Collection Is
Sought for Modern Museum." *New York Times*, 14
October 1968, p. 55.

59. Mellow, James R. "The Stein Salon Was the First
Museum of Modern Art." *New York Times*, 1
December 1968, Sec. 6, p. 48.

Mellow's article, based on the rumor that the Museum of
Modern Art and its trustees were buying the Stein collection,
traces the history of its works of art.

60. Glueck, Grace. "Modern Museum Gets Stein's Art."
    New York Times, 10 January 1969, p. 39.

    The Museum of Modern Art bought the 47-work collection,
    which contained 38 Picasso and 9 Gris, for $6-6.5 million.

61. Bloom, Ellen F. "Three Steins: A Very Personal
    Recital." *Texas Quarterly*, 13 (Summer 1970), 14-22.

    Ellen Bloom's stepfather, Julian Stein, was first cousin of
    Gertrude and her brothers and sisters. This is, therefore, really
    a "personal recollection" of the American expatriate branch
    of the family, a recollection dwelling mostly on Gertrude's visit
    to the United States and Ellen's visits with Gertrude in Paris
    shortly before Gertrude's death.

62. Glueck, Grace. "Alcoa Fund Gives $100,000 to
    Mount Stein Exhibition." *New York Times*, 7 October
    1970, p. 38.

    "Four Americans in Paris: The Collections of Gertrude Stein
    and Her Family" contained 175 works from 1905-1915. It
    also contained a gallery of "photographs and documents about
    the family and their friends."

63. ———. "The Family Knew What It Liked." *New York
    Times*, 13 December 1970, Sec. 2, p. 23.

    This could be subtitled: How Margaret Potter Got the
    Museum of Modern Art Exhibit Together.

64. Davis, Douglas. "American in Paris." *Newsweek*, 76
    (14 December 1970), 80-81B.

    Davis writes a biographically oriented article on *Four
    Americans in Paris.*

65. Hughes, R. "Patrons and Roped Climbers." *Time*,
    96 (14 December 1970), 76-81.

    The best part of this article on Cubist painters (and Cubist
    pictures in the Stein collection on exhibit at the Museum of
    Modern Art) is the section of color photos of seven works of
    art. Hughes writes about these seven and their creators.

66. Kramer, Hilton. "Paris Era Recalled in Stein Collections." *New York Times*, 18 December 1970, p. 50.

    Four Americans in Paris is "a wonderful show that reflects the special enthusiasm of the collectors."

67. Lask, Thomas. "Gertrude Stein amidst Her Talented Friends." *New York Times*, 21 December 1970, p. 71.

    The National Educational Television biography "When This You See Remember Me" is "an enticing 90 minutes," which Lask approaches as a tribute to Stein, a nostalgia-piece for the early twentieth-century, and as overly biased in Stein's favor.

68. Kramer, Hilton. "In the Heyday of the Paris Avant Garde." *New York Times*, 27 December 1970, Sec. 2, p. 25.

    Kramer gives some background information on the *Four Americans in Paris* exhibition.

69. Haverstick, Iola S. "Three Lively Ladies of the Overbury Collection." *Columbia Library Columns*, 21, No. 2 (1971), 20-27.

70. Raffel, Gertrude Stein. "There Once Was a Family Called Stein." *A Primer for the Gradual Understanding of Gertrude Stein*. Ed. Robert Bartlett Haas. Los Angeles: Black Sparrow Press, 1971. Pp. 127-38.

    Gertrude Stein Raffel looks at her mother Bertha and at her three Stein uncles and one Stein aunt.

71. Rose, Sir Francis. "Gertrude Stein: Still Leading." *Vogue*, 157 (1 January 1971), 88–89, 133 and 135.

    Rose's article contains rather malicious mistakes and is poorly written.

72. Mellow, James R. "A Crucial Stop in Paris." *New York Times*, 3 January 1971, Sec. 2, p. 19.

Obviously a preparation for *Charmed Circle* (I-B-i-9), this article concerns the salon on Rue de Fleurus and Rue Madame, and the people likely to be there.

73. Prideaux, T. "Four Patron Saints in One Great Act: The Steins." *Life*, 70 (23 April 1971), 56-60, 61-62, and 65.

74. Gervasi, Frank. "Liberation of Gertrude Stein." *Saturday Review*, 54 (21 August 1971), 13-14 and 57.

Gervasi's article is a remembrance (probably refreshed if not engendered by the NET biographical documentary) of Stein and Alice B. Toklas written some 27 years after the first and only meeting with the pair, although he later became friends with Alice (this is the impression given by Gervasi; Toklas does not mention Gervasi until June 1960[?] in a letter to Bernard Faÿ, reprinted in *Staying on Alone*). Half the article concerns Gervasi's trip with Eric Sevareid "to try to 'liberate' Gertrude Stein," who had been liberated the day before. Sevareid and Gervasi visited 1 September 1944.

Gervasi writes that he had "heard and read much about her [Stein's] unwomanliness and her lesbian relationship with Alice." Benjamin Reid, of course, refers to the lesbian relationship between Helen and Sophie (*Things As They Are*); much may have been implied, or heard, but Virgil Thomson seems to have been the first to commit the "indiscretion" openly, and in print. A minor point, surely, but my research has not opened up any references, in print, before 1944, to Gertrude and Alice's relationship.

"Those two women were genuine human beings, loving and lovable, and endowed with the gift of friendship."

75. Sutherland, Donald. "Gertrude and Alice and Others." *Prairie Schooner*, Fall 1971, pp. 284-99.

In a section from his unpublished autobiography, Sutherland remembers Stein, Alice B. Toklas and others—

Ernest Hemingway and Sutherland. Most of all, it is the
history of a series of visits Sutherland paid Toklas
between 1962 and 1965, and his hearing of her death in
1967.

76. Baker, William D., ed. *Widening Circle*, 1, No. 4
(1973).

> *Widening Circle* devotes an entire issue to Gertrude Stein as
> a special tribute.

77. Baker, William D. "Lighting Birthday Candles for
Gertrude Stein." *Widening Circle*, 1, No. 4 (1973),
1-2.

78. Gallup, Donald. "Introducing Gertrude Stein."
Widening Circle, 1, No. 4 (1973), 6-10.

> A program in Choisy-le-Roi, 4 March 1945.

79. Haas, Robert Bartlett. "A Bolt of Energy, or Why I
Still Read Gertrude Stein." *Widening Circle*, 1, No. 4
(1973), 14-17.

80. Harrison, Gilbert A. "A Remembrance." *Widening
Circle*, 1, No. 4 (1973), 18-19.

81. Meyerowitz, Patricia. "Say Yes to Everything."
Widening Circle, 1, No. 4 (1973), 20-22.

82. Rogers, W. G. "I Remember Gertrude." *Widening
Circle*, 1, No. 4 (1973), 23-24 and 30.

83. Rose, Francis. "A Gift of Roses." *Widening Circle*,
1, No. 4 (1973), 25-27.

84. Sprigge, Elizabeth. "To Begin with Beginning."
Widening Circle, 1, No. 4 (1973), 28-30.

> Sprigge tells of her discovery of Stein through *Yes Is for a
> Very Young Man. Journal in Quest of Gertrude Stein* was to have
> been published by Covent Garden Press in 1973.

85. Sutherland, Donald. "A Passion for the World."
    Widening Circle, 1, No. 4 (1973), 34-35.

    This article consists of the last three paragraphs of
    "Gertrude Stein and the Twentieth Century" (II-C-169).

86. Sutton, William A. "All Life Is Important." *Widening
    Circle*, 1, No. 4 (1973), 36-37.

87. Thomson, Virgil. "No Diminuation of Power."
    Widening Circle, 1, No. 4 (1973), 38 and 19.

    "No Diminuation of Power" is excerpted from Virgil
    Thomson's *Virgil Thomson* (I-B-ii-91).

88. Lord, James. "Where the Pictures Were: A Memoir."
    Prose, 7 (Fall 1973), 133-87.

    "I do remember the vitality, curiosity and exuberance of
    her talk." In her later years, she supported younger artists
    "who had only their personal admiration for her to offer as
    proof of creative genius. . . ." *Brewsie and Willie* "is one of her
    worst" books "because it presumes to speak for once of people
    other than herself."

89. Winant, Fran and Loretta Ulmschneider. "Gertrude
    Stein." *Women Remembered: A Collection of Biographies
    from the Furies*. Ed. Nancy Myron and Charlotte
    Bunch. Baltimore, Maryland: Diana Press, 1974.
    Pp. 63-75.

    This is a rather substandard and not totally accurate
    portrayal of Stein and Alice B. Toklas. Pages 63-70 present
    an edition of "A Sonatina Followed by Another"; of the five
    pages remaining, one is taken up by a photograph of Alice
    B. Toklas, the other four are biographical/critical.

90. Wysor, Bettie. *The Lesbian Myth: Insights and
    Conversations*. New York: Random House, 1974.

    Pages 250-52 contain a discussion of *Fernhurst* and of *Q.E.D.*
    that is superficial and inaccurate.

91. Gold, Arthur and Robert Fizdale. "How Famous
    People Cook: Alice B. Toklas." *Vogue*, 163
    (February 1974), 132-33+.

    This remembrance of Toklas includes four of her recipes
    and a consideration of *Staying on Alone*.

92. Thurman, Judith. "A Rose Is a Rose Is a Rose Is a
    Rose: Gertrude Stein." *Ms.*, February 1974, pp.
    54-57 and 93-95.

93. Anon. "Steiniana" in "Talk of the Town." *New
    Yorker*, 50 (11 March 1974), 27-29.

    This concerns an exhibition called "A Tribute to Gertrude
    Stein, 1874-1946," which contained "all of the subject's
    published writings," with books from other famous
    writers, photographs, and Stein's address book.

94. Steloff, Frances. "In Touch with Genius: Gertrude
    Stein." *Journal of Modern Literature*, 4 (April 1975),
    795-99.

    Steloff's article first appeared in *Confrontation*, 8 (Spring
    1974), 9-17.

95. Shirley, David L. "Display on World of Gertrude
    Stein." *New York Times*, 13 April 1975, p. 115.

    "30 works that . . . depict Miss Stein and her friends"
    were displayed at the C. W. Post Art Gallery exhibition,
    "Gertrude Stein and Her Friends."

II. Analytical and Critical Material

A. Critical Books and Typescripts

1. Anon. *"Pictures for a Picture" of Gertrude Stein As a Collector and Writer on Art and Artists.* New Haven: Yale University Press, 1951.

   This is a catalog of an exhibition, the nucleus of which was paintings, drawings and art objects left to Yale as the *Gertrude Stein Collection*; the exhibition included excerpts from Stein's works. The catalog contains some pictures of paintings and the history of Stein's infatuation with art, according to Stein.

2. Bridgman, Richard. *Gertrude Stein in Pieces.* New York: Oxford University Press, 1970.

   Probably the most important, indispensable, *published* Stein criticism to this date, Bridgman's examines all Stein memorabilia and works, all criticism and all biography. Considering that this is only a 340-page book (not including the appendices and a fairly complete bibliography), the shortcomings become immediately obvious: Bridgman attempts to cover too much ground in much too short a work. On the other hand, Bridgman is one of the first published critics to treat the Stein-Toklas relationship honestly. He thus admits Alice B. Toklas's importance in the creation of Stein's work.

   His exhaustive and meticulous research has enabled him, in numerous incidents, to interpret passages that were previously unexplained—and thought unexplainable—in some of Stein's works; and to forward suggestions, based on biographical information, for understanding other passages.

   The most remarkable gap in this book, and in Bridgman's other Stein writings, is one of commitment—in fact, any kind of critical opinion—to the work as a whole or "in pieces." He very ably skirts this appraisal, which leads at times to a ludicrously puritanical negligence in discussion of some lyrics and at other times to an unexplained omission of any

53

discussion whatsoever, despite Bridgman's admission of
Stein's homosexual involvement with Toklas. This reluctance
to appraise or to evaluate Stein adds an undefinable and
elusive bias to Bridgman's entire work.

At the same time, Bridgman's is a work that all Stein
scholars or students must have. One hopes that it will be a
seminal and not a definitive work.

3. Burns, Edward, ed. *Gertrude Stein on Picasso*. New York:
   Liveright, 1970.

   This very well made book commemorating the Cubists
   contains three of Stein's works on Pablo Picasso, a transcription
   of a portion of Stein's notebooks by Leon Katz, and a critical
   essay by Edward Burns and Leon Katz on Stein and Picasso.
   There are numerous photographs of Stein, of Stein's Picasso
   collection, manuscripts, Picasso, and so on. Furthermore,
   there are many printer's errors.

   That several paragraphs of "The First Making of *The Making
   of Americans*" (II-B-13) are incorporated, although
   unacknowledged, in the essay by Katz and Burns is somewhat
   understandable; that several paragraphs are incorporated in
   Burns's "Note on the Texts" is, however, another matter.

4. Copeland, Carolyn Faunce. *Language and Time and
   Gertrude Stein*. Iowa City: University of Iowa, 1975.
   See II-B-3.

5. Gordon, Irene, ed. *Four Americans in Paris: The
   Collections of Gertrude Stein and Her Family*. New York:
   The Museum of Modern Art, 1970.

   The contents of this catalog are as follows: "A World
   beyond the World: The Discovery of Leo Stein," by Irene
   Gordon (Leo's discovery of Modern Art, i.e., Paul Cezanne,
   and his subsequent pioneering, i.e., of Henri Matisse and Pablo
   Picasso); "The Michael Steins of San Francisco: Art Patrons
   and Collectors," Lucile M. Golson; "Matisse, Picasso and
   Gertrude Stein," Leon Katz (cf. II-B-13 and II-A-3, in
   particular "They Walk in the Light"); "Gertrude Stein and
   Juan Gris," Douglas Cooper; "The Cone Sisters and the Stein
   Family," Ellen B. Hirschland; "More Adventures," Leo

Stein; also, Gertrude Stein's portraits of Matisse and Picasso, photographs of the Rue de Fleurus atelier 1906-1914/15, and plates of the Stein's holdings.

The book contains an interesting account of the introduction of the Steins to art, especially modern art, of the building up and of the disposal of their collections. Katz compares and contrasts Picasso's and Stein's art and draws some conclusions about how Stein saw her art as cubistic.

6. Hoffman, Frederick J. *Gertrude Stein*. Pamphlets on American Writers, No. 10. Minneapolis: University of Minnesota Press, 1961.

Hoffman writes that, when Stein "settled in Paris (1903), at 27, rue de Fleurus, she was unknown and unpublished." This can be explained by the fact that, other than the so-called "Radcliffe themes," she had written nothing. (See, however, her two articles in *Psychological Review*.)

Perhaps one reason for the many misconceptions in Hoffman's work is that it is a short (about 40 pages) essay attempting to encompass a long and complex career.

7. Hoffman, Michael J. *The Development of Abstractionism in the Writings of Gertrude Stein*. Philadelphia: University of Pennsylvania Press, 1965.

Hoffman's book, important when it first appeared, covers the works from the first 10 years of Stein's writing career: *Q.E.D., Three Lives, Making of Americans, Tender Buttons*, and assorted portraits. Leon Katz's dissertation (II-B-13) on the *Making of Americans*, however, in many ways outdoes Hoffman's discussion of this work, and Richard Bridgman's subsequent work (II-A-2) with Stein's notebooks also dates Hoffman in some areas. On the other hand, Hoffman very carefully approaches these early works of Stein—and the Stein critics—and provides as good a basis for the further study of Stein as any of the other 1960s books. (In *Gertrude Stein*, Hoffman describes this earlier work as a "detailed account of the progressive development of Stein's characteristic style.")

8. ——. *Gertrude Stein*. Boston, Massachusetts:
   Twayne, 1976.

9. Lundell, William. Interview with Gertrude Stein on
   WJZ radio in New York on 12 November 1934,
   8:30-8:45 p.m. Typescript at Yale Collection of
   American Literature.

   Julian Sawyer describes this interview as concerning
   "Miss Stein's own writings and her reactions to the American
   scene after thirty-one years absence from the United States."

10. Miller, Rosalind. *Gertrude Stein: Form and
    Intelligibility: Containing the Radcliffe Themes*. New
    York: Exposition Press, 1949.

11. Ottawa. National Gallery of Canada. *Gertrude Stein
    & Picasso & Juan Gris*. Ottawa: La Galerie nationale du
    Canada, 1971.

    The Museum of Modern Art lent Gris, Pablo Picasso and
    Stein (*Four Americans in Paris*) to the National Gallery 25 June-
    15 August 1971. This folder consists of the catalog of the show;
    photos of Picasso's Stein, Stein's atelier, and members of
    the family; a chronology "Gertrude Stein et Pablo Picasso
    et Juan Gris à Paris 1903-1920"; three short booklets—
    Extraits de *Picasso* par Gertrude Stein, Librairie Floury,
    Paris, 1938;Gertrude Stein et Juan Gris par Douglas Cooper
    (*Four Americans in Paris*), and an introduction by Jean
    Sutherland Boggs (La Directrice de la Galerie nationale du
    Canada), "Gertrude Stein, Collectionneur." The introduction
    is very sketchy.
    "L'exposition d'Ottawa comprend seulement les tableaux
    que Gertrude Stein a gardés jusqu'à sa mort dans sa
    collection, ceux des deux artistes qu'elle admirait le plus:
    Pablo Picasso et Juan Gris."

12. Reid, Benjamin. *Art by Subtraction: A Dissenting Opinion of Gertrude Stein*. Norman: University of Oklahoma Press, 1958.

Reid's was the first book-length attempt to deal with Stein's work adversely. That is, he begins critically, logically, but quickly descends into subjective vindictiveness (e.g., p. 74: "Although it is hard to believe that Gertrude Stein did not have some such experience as that of Adele—the book is tinged with that degree of intimacy which always suggests autobiographical sources—one cannot, of course, impugn her sexuality. . . ").

13. Rose, Francis (Sir Francis Cyril Rose). *Gertrude Stein and Painting*. London: Book Collecting and Library Monthly, 1968.

The preface, by Alice B. Toklas, was written in 1963 (September). Rose's book contains factual errors as well as misspellings. He writes, for example, that Natalie Barney was a regular of Stein's salon, an insupportable statement. It is known that Stein visited Barney's salon, that the two women were friends and went walking together, but it is impossible to trace Rose's statement.

14. Russell, Francis. *Three Studies in Twentieth Century Obscurity*. Aldington, Kent: Hand and Flower Press, 1954.

Stein "was the first writer in English to express fully the disintegrative tendencies that have been the hall-mark of advanced western art movements from the latter part of the nineteenth century." Russell goes on, in some fifty-plus pages, to compare Stein's writings to the gibberish of a child: "In the plays and portraits it is the infantile repetitions, the echoes and counting-out rhymes, the stringing of words together the way a four-year-old strings wooden beads. In her autobiographies and war reflections the style and thought currents and general attitude are those of a wide-eyed child." Mr. Russell is not complimenting Stein here; he goes on to say that she carried this "retreat from reason" (shared by the surrealists, German expressionists and Dadaists) "to the point where a child first becomes aware of words and sits mouthing them over and over again as if tasting their quality, unaware of the meaning but delighting in the process."

Russell criticizes *Three Lives, Making of Americans, Things As They Are, Tender Buttons,* some of the portraits and plays in *Geography and Plays,* the two autobiographies, and *Wars I Have Seen.*

15. Stewart, Allegra. *Gertrude Stein and the Present.* Cambridge, Massachusetts: Harvard University Press, 1967.

This is a Jungian study of Stein's oeuvre. As such it presents innumerable difficulties to the "average" reader. Large sections were completely incomprehensible to me—much more so than Stein herself. On the other hand, some of Stewart's insights into the makeup and the motivation of Stein's pieces are enlightening. An entire chapter is devoted to *Tender Buttons* and one to *Doctor Faustus Lights the Lights.* Despite the problems of the reader without the vocabulary, Stewart offers something to the serious Stein student that had not previously been offered: a serious, intensely philosophical trip into Gertrude Stein. See "The Quality of Gertrude Stein's Creativity," *American Literature,* 28 (1957), 488-506.

16. Sutherland, Donald. *Gertrude Stein: A Biography of Her Work.* New Haven: Yale University Press, 1951.

This is the first book-length study of Stein's work. As such, it provides a basis, a jumping-off point for later studies of Stein. Sutherland, however, is adamantly pro-Stein, a bias which detracts from the objectivity of the book; he also tends (subconsciously or unconsciously) to imitate Stein's style.

17. Weinstein, Norman. *Gertrude Stein and the Literature of the Modern Consciousness.* New York: Ungar, 1970.

First of all Weinstein's book contains misspellings ('Steward' instead of 'Stewart', for example), a very inconsistent bibliographical form, and footnotes which are not supported by a "bibliography" entry.

Secondly, and most importantly, Weinstein attempts to approach a study of Stein through linguistics. He looks, of course, at "Melanctha," *Tender Buttons* and *The Making of Americans,* but he also discusses *Stanzas in Meditation* and *Four Saints in Three Acts.* Weinstein's bias—in favor of Stein—is ever-present; despite that, he presents a very objective look at Stein, her theories and her works, and presents many suggestions—a number of which are new—to reading and understanding Stein.

B. Dissertations

1. Blomme, Gayle Campbell Barnes. "Gertrude Stein's Concepts of the Self and Her Literary Characters." Diss. University of Michigan 1973.

   Blomme writes about the function of the "human being," especially in *Three Lives, Making of Americans* and *Portraits and Prayers*. She is also concerned with the place of the narrator and the identity of the narrator in various works. There is much summarization and quotation of Stein. The "Concepts of Self" mentioned in the dissertation title are psychologically based.

2. Caserio, Robert Lawrence, Jr. "Plot, Story and the Novel: Problematic Aspects of English and American Narrative, from Dickens to Gertrude Stein." Diss. Yale University 1973.

3. Copeland, Carolyn Faunce. "Narrative Techniques in the Works of Gertrude Stein." Diss. University of Iowa 1973.

   An interesting study of the development of the narrator's role in Stein's works, Copeland's dissertation was published as *Language and Time and Gertrude Stein* (Iowa City: University of Iowa Press, 1975).

4. Davis, Eric Hunter. "Gertrude Stein's Return to Narrative." Diss. Harvard University 1970.

5. DeKoven, Marianne. "Explaining Gertrude Stein: A Criticism for Experimental Style." Diss. Stanford University 1976.

   DeKoven is interested in avant-garde writing and studies Stein's styles from 1906 through 1932, especially the experimental work.

6. Dubnick, Randa Kay. "Gertrude Stein and Cubism: A Structural Analysis of Obscurity." Diss. University of Colorado at Boulder 1976.

7. Edgington, K. Ann. "Abstraction As a Concept in the Criticism of Gertrude Stein and Wassily Kandinsky." Diss. American University 1976.

     This dissertation is "a metacritical examination of the use of abstraction as a critical concept by literary critics writing about Gertrude Stein. . . ."

8. Fendelman, Earl. "Toward a Third Voice: Autobiographical Form in Thoreau, Stein, Adams, and Mailer." Diss. Yale University 1971.

     Chapter 2 of Fendelman's dissertation is "Gertrude Stein: The Self and Art" (pp. 78-140).

9. Friedling, Sheila. "Problems of Perception in the Modern Novel: The Representation of Consciousness in Works of Henry James, Gertrude Stein and William Faulkner." Diss. University of Wisconsin 1973.

     Friedling refers to *Three Lives* as a modern novel in Chapter 5, "Gertrude Stein: Temporal Modes of Consciousness and Narration." She also comments "Stein refers in her autobiography" (?). There is much repetition; the abstract and preface are practically the same, and parts of the preface are repeated in the text. Among other things, each section of *Three Lives* is underlined.

10. Garvin, Harry Raphael. "Gertrude Stein: A Study of Her Theory and Practice." Diss. University of Michigan 1950.

     N.B. Richard Bridgman, in *Gertrude Stein in Pieces* (II-A-2), and Michael J. Hoffman, in *Gertrude Stein* (II-A-8), list this as being completed in 1949.

11. Hoffman, Michael J. "The Development of Abstractionism in the Writings of Gertrude Stein to 1913." Diss. University of Pennsylvania 1964.

     See II-A-7.

12. Howitt, Wayne Andrew. "Reading As a Creative Effort: A Study Utilizing Gertrude Stein's *Tender Buttons.*" Diss. State University of New York at Buffalo 1974.

> Howitt reviews the "origins of *Tender Buttons* and the particular internal features of the book which necessitates a continuous reaction by the reader." His chronology is sometimes wrong. This is a somewhat far-fetched discussion, based on "Stein's combination of interests in . . . psychology, meditation, and literature."

13. Katz, Leon. "The First Making of *The Making of Americans:* A Study Based on Gertrude Stein's Notebooks and Early Versions of Her Novel (1902-1908)." Diss. Columbia University 1963.

> To quote Richard Bridgman in *Gertrude Stein in Pieces* (II-A-2): "For an understanding of Gertrude Stein's preliminary drafts of *The Making of Americans* I have relied upon Leon Katz's invaluable dissertation . . . which is based upon an analysis of Gertrude Stein's unpublished notebooks, drafts of the novel, and extensive interviews with her contemporaries." Katz also refers extensively to other works by Stein, for instance *Three Lives, Q.E.D., A Long Gay Book* and *The Autobiography of Alice B. Toklas.* The fact that he has access to the notebooks (and is preparing an edition of them), and that he provides a very thorough look at Stein's early works and a very strong background for them, makes his work indispensable to Stein scholars.

14. Leach, Wilford. "Gertrude Stein and the Modern Theatre." Diss. University of Illinois 1956.

> Mr. Leach has written a doctoral dissertation on "Stein's concepts of dramaturgy and the theatre, and the relationship of these concepts to her belief that her art manifested the 'composition' of twentieth century existence."

15. Lowe, Frederick W., Jr. "Gertrude's Web: A Study of Gertrude Stein's Literary Relationships." Diss. Columbia University 1957.

16. McMeniman, Linda Jeanne. "Design and Experiment in *The Making of Americans* by Gertrude Stein." Diss. University of Pennsylvania 1976.

   McMeniman deals with authorial intrusion in and the structure of *The Making of Americans*, "a critique" of "American middle-class life."

17. McMillan, Samuel Hubert, Jr. "Gertrude Stein, the Cubists, and the Futurists." Diss. University of Texas 1964.

   Of especial interest is McMillan's "Appendix: Gertrude Stein Criticism—Some Opinions." The main difficulty with this section is, however, the retreat in the last paragraph from the very good point he was developing throughout the 15 pages of the appendix. In his first paragraph McMillan writes "that the treatments of [Stein's] work usually lose a sense of objectivity." He then treats several important critics. In the next to last sentence of this section, after pointing out the basic weaknesses of these criticisms, McMillan excuses himself for criticizing the critics: "The difficulties of critics . . . are perhaps partially accountable in what might be called a tendency in human nature to defend a reasonable position beyond the limitations of objectivity."

18. Roe, Nancy Ellen. "Gertrude Stein: Rhetoric and the 'Modern Composition'." Diss. University of Michigan 1971.

19. Sayre, Henry Marshall. "A World Unsuspected: Gertrude Stein, William Carlos Williams, and the Rise of American Modernism." Diss. University of Washington 1976.

   Chapter 1, "The Example of Gertrude Stein," is the main section of Stein; the rest deals with her influence on Williams and his reactions.

20. Schoonover, David Eugene. "The Long Way Home: American Literary Expatriates in Paris, 1919-1929." Diss. Princeton University 1975.

    Chapter 1 is on Gertrude Stein, who "bridge[d] expatriate generations." Other chapters deal with Sherwood Anderson, Ernest Hemingway and F. Scott Fitzgerald.

21. Steiner, Wendy Lois. "Gertrude Stein's Portrait Form." Diss. Yale University 1974.

    Steiner's dissertation will be published by Yale University Press.

22. Thigpen, Janet. "A Manual for Teaching Counselor Trainees Existential Concepts through an Exploration of the Life and Writings of Gertrude Stein." Diss. East Texas State University 1971.

23. Walker, Jayne Lee. "Gertrude Stein and Her Objects: From 'Melanctha' to *Tender Buttons*." Diss. University of California, Berkeley 1975.

    The main works Walker studies are *Three Lives* (and *Q.E.D.*), *Tender Buttons*, *Two*, *GMP*, and *Making of Americans*. She points out the parallels between Pablo Picasso's and Stein's developments and the changes in Stein's attitudes toward the "objects" "she wished to represent."

C. Critical Articles, Chapters of Books, and Critical Mentions

1. Van Vechten, Carl. "How to Read Gertrude Stein."
   Trend, 7 (August 1914), 553-57.

2. Aldington, Richard. "Disciples of Gertrude Stein."
   Poetry, 17 (October 1920), 35-40.

   Aldington speaks of Edgar Allan Poe's "The Raven,"
   Walt Whitman's *Leaves of Grass*, and Stein's *Tender Buttons* as
   "three impingements of American genius upon the mind
   of Europe." He does, however, treat the Dadaists as the
   French disciples of Stein, with Guillaume Apollinaire the first French
   apostle, and writes that they are marked by "obscurity of
   diction, extreme fragility of thought, a pleasing vacuum in
   place of a subject, and typographical excesses."

3. Anderson, Sherwood. "Four American Impressions."
   New Republic, 32 (11 October 1922), 171.

   Containing no concrete criticism of Gertrude Stein,
   Anderson's article approaches Stein sentimentally, as
   "old brick houses with immense old-fashioned kitchens—
   in which I loved to linger," except that Stein "is a worker in
   words with the same living touch in her strong fingers that
   was characteristic of the women of the kitchens of the brick
   houses in the town of my boyhood."
   Building upon his discussion of words in "Work of
   Gertrude Stein" (II-D-1), Anderson describes Stein as "laying
   word against word, relating sound to sound, feeling for
   the taste, the smell, the rhythm of the individual word."
   Anderson felt that Stein's literary work would end up of
   more importance to English-language writers than any more
   comprehensible writer.

4. Wilson, Edmund. "A Guide to Gertrude Stein."
   Vanity Fair, September 1923, pp. 60 and 80.

   Wilson is concerned mainly with *Three Lives*, "one of the
   most distinguished works of fiction by any living American
   author. . . ." *Three Lives* belongs to Stein's first period;

History of a Family to her "middle manner"; *Tender Buttons* to a
third (?) style. Works like *Geography and Plays* and *Have
They Attacked Mary* consist of all of Stein's styles. Stein's
strength lies in "her grasp of character." "There is, perhaps,
no other American writer of importance who has been so
badly underestimated as Gertrude Stein. . . ."

5. Anon. "Gertrude Stein and a Robin." *Atlantic Monthly,*
   133 (March 1924), 427-28.

   A typical early criticism, short, negative and sarcastic,
   this one compares Stein to a robin: "There was the desire—if
   not the capacity—to tell a story, and to do it, not simply, but
   with the nuances of unintelligibility, symphonies of
   monotonous notes, *bravuras* of aimless repetition."

6. Loy, Mina. "Gertrude Stein." *Transatlantic Review,*
   2 (October 1924), 305-09; 427-30.

   Loy, in an early attempt to explain Stein, is mostly
   concerned with explication of several pieces from *Geography
   and Plays.*

7. Graves, Robert. *Contemporary Techniques of Poetry: A
   Political Analogy.* Hogarth Essay No. 8. London: The
   Hogarth Press, 1925.

   Graves's essay deals with the different "parties" embroiled
   in the reclassification of "Rules of Poetry." He makes it a
   political analogy by referring to the right, left, liberals,
   conservatives. Stein is a liberal-anarchist. "Extreme anarchy
   is represented by Miss Gertrude Stein, author of *Tender
   Buttons, Three Lives, Geography and Plays.*"
   "I must confess that I have great respect for this work; it
   is nonsense, but only according to a narrow classification of
   sense. To disregard it is not altogether a sign of mental
   strength and activity: [here follows a quote, ending:] 'The
   way to say it, is to say it.'
   "And certainly Miss Stein says it and says it sincerely."
   (This ends the section on diction.)

8. Sitwell, Edith. *Poetry and Criticism*. Hogarth Essays No. 11. London: The Hogarth Press, 1925.

   "Miss Stein is bringing back life to our language by what appears, at first, to be an anarchic process. First she breaks down the predestined groups of words, their sleepy family habits; then she rebrightens them, examines their textures, and builds them into new and vital shapes."

9. Crockett, Mary. "Gertrude Stein." *Modern Quarterly*, 2, No. 3 (1925), 233-37.

   Modern Quarterly is a "journal of radical opinion," which "advances the sociological approach to literature, philosophy and science. Its outlook is that of historical materialism. . . ."

10. Forster, E.M. *Aspects of the Novel*. London: Arnold, 1927.

    Stein "tried to abolish time" and failed. "She has hoped to emancipate fiction from the tyranny of time and to express in it the life by values only. She fails, because as soon as fiction is completely delivered from time it cannot express anything at all. . . . There is nothing to ridicule in such an experiment as hers. It is much more important to play about like this than to rewrite the Waverley Novels. Yet the experiment is doomed to failure. The time-sequence cannot be destroyed without carrying in its ruin all that should have taken its place; the novel that would express values only becomes unintelligible and therefore valueless."

11. Rodker, John. *The Future of Futurism*. New York: E.P. Dutton, 1927.

    In "Attempts to Revitalize the Language," Rodker writes that Stein's "words are arranged not so much in free association, for their relation is obvious, but as though they were units and interdependent, and they are developed in recurring motifs as a fugue might be developed. . . ." Here is "an extravagant method" and an "ungrateful method" in which "words [are] to be words only and to mean nothing but what she would have them mean."

12. Canby, Henry Seidel. "Gyring and Gimbling."
    Saturday Review, 30 April 1927, p. 777. Reprinted in
    Henry Seidel Canby, *American Estimates*. New York:
    Harcourt, Brace, 1929. Pp. 170-77.

    This article concerns James Joyce's *Finnegans Wake* (a
    portion of which is included) and Stein's "An Elucidation"
    (printed in its entirety), which "is an onslaught and ravage
    upon the English language which hitherto has been able to
    combine the highest imagination with sense, common and
    uncommon."

13. Riding, Laura. "The New Barbarism and Gertrude
    Stein." *transition*, June 1927, pp. 153-68.

14. Lewis, Wyndham. *Time and Western Man*. New York:
    Harcourt, Brace, 1928.

    In Chapter 10, "Tests for Counterfeit in the Arts," Lewis
    discusses *Composition As Explanation*.

15. Riding, Laura and Robert Graves. *A Survey of
    Modernist Poetry*. New York: Doubleday, Doran, 1928.

    "Gertrude Stein is perhaps the only artisan of language
    who has ever succeeded in practising scientific barbarism
    literally. Her words are primitive in that they are bare,
    immobile, mathematically placed, abstract. . . ."

16. Rosenfeld, Paul. "The Place of Gertrude Stein."
    *By Way of Art: Criticisms of Music, Literature, Painting,
    Sculpture, and the Dance*. New York: Coward McCann,
    1928. Pp. 111-31. Originally appeared in *Saturday
    Review*, 2 January 1926.

    Rosenfeld describes Stein's as "a personal democratic
    American literature not in imitation but in the intention
    of Walt Whitman." He writes further of "the retrospective
    discovery [!] of her place in the new literature, the
    appreciation of her work. . . . Her first volume not a whit
    less than her last exhibits her manful and constant effort to
    set down with the aid of words the pattern, the motion of
    volumes, established in her by her subject-matters. . . ." As

early as the *Camera Work* portraits Stein "uncompromisingly
set appropriate vocabularies to the task of describing a
number of volumes in combinations, dispositions and
sequences expressive of her relations to the two subjects
[Pablo Picasso and Henry Matisse], and representative of
what they meant to her. . . ."

Rosenfeld sees three stages of development in the work
of Gertrude Stein. The first is represented by "Melanctha"
and *Three Lives*: "Language used in the interest of
description is here balanced with language used primarily
for the purpose of communicating the direct feeling of
things, the rhythmical pattern created in the author by her
object." The second stage includes *Making of Americans*,
"short stories, Ada, Miss Furr and Miss Skeene, A Family
of Perhaps Three; [by] the famous essays on Matisse and Picasso
and the less famous ones on [Georges] Braque and Italians;
and [by] the series of portraits. . . . It commences with a
mere sharpening and essentialization of the method
developed in Three Lives. . . . Soundings for the mystical
roots of characters have gone deeper, and the findings have
been confided more sheerly to the conduct of the prose. . . ."
The third period has its beginnings in *Tender Buttons*, "the
least interesting and rewarding of her published pieces . . ."
and "a further development took the form of the baffling
lists included in Geography and Plays." This period is just
beginning; it won't last.

17. Schmalhausen, Samuel D. "Gertrude Stein, Or,
    Light on the Literary Aspects of Enuresis." *Modern
    Quarterly*, 5, No. 3 (1928-1930), 313-23.

18. Church, Ralph. "A Note on the Writings of Gertrude
    Stein." *transition*, 14 (Fall 1928), 164-68.

    This appears to be a philosophical criticism by an Oxford
    student. Church approaches Stein's writing not because
    of its poetic qualities but because of its quality of being
    "self contained."

    "What Miss Stein says derives its meaning from nothing
    external to her writing, but from her realization of what she
    presents in, rather than merely suggests by, her words. . . .

What it says is given in no tenuous references to an external subject, but in the presented character of the writing itself." He defends Stein's writing by differentiating between "discursive" and "final" writing. Stein's is final (which explains the many bad reviews)—"of what she writes, Miss Stein realizes something of its nature and she is able perhaps to express that directly in words."

19. Munson, Gorham B. "Prose for Experimentation: Gertrude Stein." *Style and Form in American Prose.* New York: Doubleday, Doran, 1929. Pp. 278-91.

"Miss Furr and Miss Skeene" is reprinted here.

"The reader is entitled, so I hold, to be hostile to the impertinences of self-expression, but toward the literary laboratory *per se* he has no just reason for antagonism. He may be indifferent about it or he may be curious to examine its experiments, but only if he is unreasonably prejudiced vs. the new can he fly into anger." However, "we touch here a fairly persistent fallacy, the belief that words can produce effects proper to the other arts. . . ."

20. Noyes, Alfred. "An Interlude." *Opalescent Parrot: Essays.* London: Sheed and Ward, 1929. Pp. 51-54.

Obviously a man with a classical bent (other essays are on John Bunyan, John Milton, William Shakespeare, Thomas Carlyle, John Keats, Francis Bacon), Noyes somehow manages to fit in this "interlude" on Stein and an essay on Walt Whitman.

21. Riding, Laura. *Experts Are Puzzled.* London: Cape, 1930.

22. Williams, William Carlos. "The Work of Gertrude Stein." *Pagany,* 1 (Winter [January-March] 1930), 41-46.

See II-G-10-11.

23. Brion, Marcel. "Le Contrepoint poètique de
Gertrude Stein." *Echanges*, 3 (June 1930), 122-28.

Referring to Stein's work, Brion writes: "Par sa rigidité,
sa dureté, son absence de nuances, de clair obscur et de
subconscient, elle représente, symétriquement sur le plan
poétique, une opération semblable à ce qu'est la fugue de
Bach sur le plan musical. Contenue tout entière an elles-même,
n'attendant rien du reflet ou de l'écho, achevée et durcie au
moment où elle s'exprime, suivant dans son développement
des arabesques qui obéissent à leur propre logique, et non à
celle des pensées et des sentiments, la poésie de Gertrude
Stein, dans son *contrepoint verbal*, obéit au même désir de
construction abstraite et d'expression intégrale qu'une fugue
de Bach dans l'ordre musical ou une arabesque de l'Alhambra
dans l'ordre plastique."

Stein *uses* words, and Brion explains and extends this
idea throughout his article. On p. 125: "Cette poésie abstraite,
volontaire, hyperconsciente, est à l'opposé de celle des
surréalistes. . . ."

24. Eastman, Max. "The Cult of Unintelligibility."
The Literary Mind: Its Place in an Age of Science. New York:
Scribner's, 1931. Pp. 57-78.

Eastman uses I.A. Richard's definition of poetry as "an
act of communication" in discussing Hart Crane, e.e.
cummings, James Joyce, Stein and Edith Sitwell. He likes
the tendency "toward the cultivation of pure poetry" but
not toward a "Cult of Unintelligibility."

25. Wilson, Edmund. "Gertrude Stein." *Axel's Castle:
A Study in the Imaginative Literature of 1870-1930*. New
York: Scribner's, 1931. Chapter 7.

Wilson's chapter contains some false implications; in speaking of
Tender Buttons, for example, Wilson writes that "Miss Stein
had by this time [1914] gone to live in Paris. . . ."

Tender Buttons, Three Lives and *The Making of Americans*
receive most of Wilson's attention, although he does mention
Geography and Plays and *Useful Knowledge*. Wilson praises
Stein for "the closeness with which the author has been able to

identify herself with her characters" in *Three Lives*. "In a
style which appears to owe nothing to that of any other novelist,
she seems to have caught the very rhythms and accents of
the minds of her heroines. . . ." Stein has a very good idea
of what makes up human personality.

Concerning *The Making of Americans*, Wilson writes: "I
confess that I have not read this book all through, and I do
not know whether it is possible to do so."

Wilson concludes that her present work is too unintelligible,
although her presence in American literature will be continually
felt on the strength of her early work.

26. MacCarthy, Desmond. "Gertrude Stein." *Criticism*.
New York: Putman, 1932. Pp. 260-72.

MacCarthy discusses *Composition As Explanation* and blames
not Miss Stein "for indulging in automatic writing," but
those who persuade her to continue and to publish.

27. Anon. "A Great Stylist Reappears." *New York Times*,
15 July 1932, p. 14.

This piece on "Scenery and George Washington: A Novel or
a Play," which appeared in the July-September 1932 *Hound
and Horn*, sees Stein as the "most original of American authors."
"Hers is the school of reorganization. She reassembles,
transforms and enchants."

28. MacDiarmid, Hugh (Christopher Murray Grieve).
"Gertrude Stein." *At the Sign of the Thistle*. London:
Stanley Nott, 1934. Pp. 33-56.

MacDiarmid writes that Anton Tchekov's "clearness" can
be found unadulterated only in Stein. He quotes several
contemporary news articles: one appearing in *Glasgow Herald*
(1922?) and one in the *Irish Statesman* on *The Making of
Americans*. MacDiarmid's preoccupation with Stein tends
towards a rather radical 1930s defense.

The Making of Americans and Gertrude Stein's work in
general, represents a wholesome dissatisfaction with all
the innumerable divergencies of literature which go nowhere
so far as the mass of mankind is concerned, a determination
to reject all such auto-deceptions of the mind and

concentrate, or, rather reconcentrate, on the essence of our psychical plight, and what T.E. Hulme said of the necessary preliminary preparation for an understanding of the religious attitude can be applied to Miss Stein's work, regarded as spadework, pioneering, towards a dynamic literature—a literature that will do what literature has never done in the past, act directly on general consciousness, circumvent all these elements which have hitherto protected the inertia, the refusal to think, to experience. . . .

The "principal value" of Stein's work "perhaps lies in its rejection of what Hulme called 'the bastard conception of personality'."

29. Sitwell, Edith. *Aspects of Modern Poetry*. London: Duckworth, 1934.

In "Notes on Innovations in Prose," Sitwell credits Stein as responsible for "the anarchic breaking up and rebuilding of sleepy families of words and phrases." "Miss Stein's power over rhythm is of an extraordinary complexity and subtlety, and by the means of rhythm she conveys all the different shades of character in the persons she evolves before our eyes. . . ." "She does not give us a logical chain of events, she gives us a state of being. . . ."

See also "Three Women Writers" (*Vogue*, 64, No. 7 [early October 1924], pp. 81 and 114) on Katherine Mansfield, Gertrude Stein and Dorothy Richardson; and "The Work of Gertrude Stein" (*Vogue*, 66, No. 7 [early October 1925], pp. 73 and 98).

30. Skinner, B.F. "Has Gertrude Stein a Secret?" *Atlantic Monthly*, 153 (January 1934), 50-57.

Skinner's is a very important early criticism which has had to be dealt with (usually very ineptly) by every Stein scholar.

31. Anon. "Two Steins." *New York Times*, 1 January 1934, p. 22.

An editorial on B.F. Skinner's article, this short Steinian defense is based on A.E. Housman's "meaning is of the intellect; poetry is not."

32. Anderson, Sherwood. "Gertrude Stein." *American Spectator*, 2 (April 1934), 3. Reprinted in Sherwood Anderson, *No Swank*. Philadelphia: Centaur Press, 1934. Pp. 81-85.

Implying that Stein is a writer's writer, Anderson tries to deal with B.F.Skinner's charges: "if you think the same result can be accomplished by any one trying automatic writing, try it. If you happen to be a person of real talent, with a feeling for words, word relationships, word color, you may get something that will surprise and please you."

Anderson is more concerned with his approaches to, with what he thinks of, the art of writing, which "is, in a sense, automatic. . . . There is something stored within that flows out." Stein is a "releaser of talent," "a path-finder." She tried "to awaken in all of us who write a new feeling for words. She has done it." She is a "revolutionist" and "a restorer of 'the word'."

33. Kirnon, Hodge. "Seeing Difference." *New York Times*, 2 November 1934, p. 22.

This is a letter reacting to Stein's statements on Negroes in her 25 October interview.

34. Anon. "Perfecting Language." *New York Times*, 19 November 1934, p. 16.

An editorial on Stein's punctuation and grammar experimentation, this article asks: why dismiss some marks of punctuation, some parts of grammar, and not others?

35. Schneider, Isidor. "Home Girl Makes Good." *New Masses*, 13 (27 November 1934), 21-22.

New Masses was a Marxist publication. Schneider reports on an interview with Stein in New York; he mentions Stein's "evasion of direct thinking."

36. Anon. "Palilalia and Gertrude Stein." *Journal of the American Medical Association*, 103 (1 December 1934), 1711-12.

This interesting approach to a phenomenon is partially

based (particularly in its literary criticism) on B.F. Skinner's "Has Gertrude Stein a Secret?"

Those familiar with such symptoms as automatic writing, palilalia, perseveration and verbigeration are inclined to wonder whether or not the literary abnormalities in which she [Stein] indulges represent correlated distortions of the intellect, or whether the entire performance is in the nature of a hoax, and that Miss Stein produces her literary effusions with her tongue in her cheek. Palilalia is a form of speech disorder in which the patient repeats many times a word, a phrase or a sentence which he has just spoken. In addition, the speech tends to be uttered more and more quickly and less distinctly. . . .

An analogous condition is palilogia, a term sometimes applied to that form of rhetoric whereby the word or sentence is deliberately repeated for purposes of emphasis. Then there is also verbal perseveration, with the same word or phrase repeated as though the original idea persisted for an undue length of time in the patient's mind to the exclusion of fresh incoming ideas. Sometimes there is echolalia, in which the patient repeats the statements or questions that have been put to him. Finally there is verbigeration, a frequent symptom in dementia praecox, in which the patient repeats the same sentence over and over.

In addition, and based upon Skinner's article and Leon M. Solomon's and Gertrude Stein's "Normal Motor Automatism" (*Psychological Review*, September 1896), the *Journal* is quick to adopt the view that "the writing of Miss Stein, such as appears in her plays, books and poems, is quite the same as she developed when experimenting with spontaneous automatic writing."

37. ———. "Stein Again." *Art Digest*, 9 (15 December 1934), 9.

This is a reiteration of Alsop's "In Words Gertrude Stein Finds Emotions" (II-E-xiii-4) and of the *New York Herald Tribune's* interpretation of the *Journal of the American Medical Association's* article (see previous entry).

38. Deutsch, Babette. *This Modern Poetry*. New York: Norton, 1935.

Stein's "strong sense of rhythm is abrogated by her lack of feeling for verbal texture. Music bores her. She has an interest in the metaphysics of language which leads her to emphasize words like 'as', 'and', 'or', representing abstract relations, and to prefer participles, with their suggestions of continuity. . . ."

39. Nathan, George Jean. *Passing Judgments*. New York: Knopf, 1935.

In the latter sixth of Chapter 11, "Several Writers for the Theatre—and Miss Stein," Miss Stein is discussed. Some of her words are "not only lacking in rhythm and pleasant sound but . . . [they are] painfully cacophonous."

Nathan argues with Stein's theory "that the meaning and sense of words placed together is of no importance; that it is only their sound and rhythm that count" because what she writes lacks "rhythm and pleasant sound"; "she every now and then halts abruptly . . . and writes some such grammatically orthodox, clear and simple sentence" (i.e., she is insincere); Nathan is disturbed because Stein cannot combine sound and meaning.

40. Anon. "Literary Snobbery." *New York Times*, 6 February 1935, p. 18.

In this editorial, Stein and James Joyce are both members of a "cult of obscurity." Stein writes the way she does to protect "a vested interest."

41. Williams, William Carlos. "A 1 Pound Stein." *The Rocking Horse* (Madison, Wisconsin), 2, No. 3 (Spring 1935), 3-5.

Ezra Pound and Stein were "both at work upon a fundamental regeneration of thought in our language." "It's the disinfecting effect of the Stein manner or better said perhaps, its releasing force, that I wish to dwell upon."

42. Braque, Georges et al. "Testimony against Gertrude Stein." *transition*, 23 (July 1935), supplement.

This very famous and hard to obtain article contains statements by Georges Braque, Eugene Jolas, Maria Jolas, Henri Matisse, André Salmon and Tristan Tzara correcting, refuting and lashing out at *The Autobiography of Alice B. Toklas*.

43. Anon. "Passion in Literature." *New York Times*, 25 August 1935, Sec. 4, p. 8.

This editorial uses an interview with Stein—and her reference to Ralph Waldo Emerson as a passionate writer—as an introduction to a discussion on passion.

44. Faÿ, Bernard. "Gertrude Stein, poète de l'Amérique." *Revue de Paris*, 42 (15 November 1935), 294-312.

Although Faÿ is an historian, he definitely should never be considered as one of Stein's biographers or critics. The article has many misquotes. Somehow, Faÿ manages to write these reminiscences without mentioning Leo or any of the other family members.

45. Gold, Michael. *Change the World!* New York: International Publishers, 1936.

"Most of these selections were first published as columns in the *Daily Worker*. Others are reprinted from the *New Masses*. . . ."

"Gertrude Stein: A Literary Idiot" appears between pp. 23 and 26. "In essence, what Gertrude Stein's work represents is an example of the most extreme subjectivism of the contemporary bourgeois artist, and a reflection of the ideological anarchy into which the whole of bourgeois literature has fallen." Her insanity is deliberate and "arises out of a false conception of the nature of art and of the function of language."

Marxists "see in the work of Gertrude Stein extreme symptoms of the decay of capitalist culture. They view her work as the complete attempt to annihilate all relations between the artist and the society in which he lives. They see in her work the same kind of orgy and spiritual abandon that marks the life of the whole leisure class."

46. Laughlin, James, IV. "About Bilignin and Literature and the GBB." *Gotham Book Mart Catalogue,* 36 (1936), 1-2, 26-28.

47. Eagleson, Harvey. "Gertrude Stein: Method in Madness." *Sewanee Review,* 44 (April-June 1936), 164-77.

   Sewanee Review abstracts the article as follows: "The theme of this is suggested in the author's sub-title: 'Method in Madness'. It is a thoughtful, scholarly, and yet thoroughly analytical study of the work of an American author who is caviare to the general. The author reaches the conclusion that 'this (Gertrude Stein's work) will never do', but the conclusion is based on something other than the conventional explosion of those who over-exert their sentiments in disposing of Miss Stein."
   Eagleson says that Stein's "influence on the arts, both graphic and literary, has been too great and too extensive for her work to be overlooked by the critic and the historian treating our period, or to be dismissed with a casual wave of the hand as semi-humorous nonsense, beneath contempt." His suggestions are, first, that Stein's works should be read aloud in order to realize the (American) rhythms and sounds; secondly, that repetition is used as a rhythmic device, a leitmotiv attempt, and also as "an attempt to express an intricate and difficult philosophical idea" concerning time, i.e., that the present is the only segment of time that exists in actuality. Therefore composition, in order to be valid, must present the present which, because it becomes the past, demands a kind of cyclic repetition.

48. Haldance, C. "Gentlemen Prefer." *English Review,* 62 (May 1936), 528.

49. Lane, James W. "The Craze for Craziness." *Catholic World,* 144 (December 1936), 306-09.

   The honor of starting the "craze for craziness" is given to Virgil Thomson and Stein's *Four Saints in Three Acts.* In attempting to combat the evils of modernism, Lane chooses sarcasm as his weapon. He has probably read William S. Knickerbocker (II-E-xi-10); "the craze for craziness" is compared to the Emperor's New Clothes.

50. Laughlin, James, IV. "New Words for Old: Notes on Experimental Writing." *Story*, December 1936, pp. 105-10.

51. Flint, F. Cudworth. "Contemporary Criticism." *Southern Review*, 2 (1936-37), 208-24.

The section concerned with Stein's *Narration* appears between pp. 208 and 213.

"Her incidental comments on the general effects produced by words in successive periods of English literature . . . exemplify her possibly unique sense for an aspect of language only to be adumbrated by some such phrase as 'the movement of words'."

"No other writer of whom I know, has made the distinction between the quality of words in Elizabethan times and their quality in the eighteenth century so evident and even . . . *tactile*, as she has done in her *Lectures in America*." Against the insights are the effects ("stultifying") of "her attempt to *arrest* time in language." Stein errs in implying that literature erects a "structural representative of itself" in the reader's mind as the work is read. Practically, by writing "as if the whole work were *at each point* in the work completely present," she errs. Stylistically, "her lectures represent a mitigation of her creative practice." "*In her lectures*" her "written style" is usually an imitation of her "spoken style."

"Some of her repetition for emphasis justifies itself. And her casting her remarks throughout in a simple language, avoiding most technical terms even in dealing with technical matters . . . has . . . the merit of forcing one to consider afresh some problem which has become stale by the familiarity of the technical language currently used in its statement and solution. On the other hand, Miss Stein . . . invariably lingers at that [a new] point too long. . . ." The result is "stupefaction."

52. Brown, Sterling Allen. *The Negro in American Fiction.*
Bronze Booklet No. 6. Washington, D.C.: The
Associates in Negro Folk Education, 1937.

> In the one-paragraph discussion of "Melanctha," in which
> both Carl Van Vechten and the short story are quoted, Brown
> says "Melanctha" is "a slowly unwound character study."
> "The characters talk in a mannered dialogue; they all sound
> like each other, and like the white people in the other two
> stories." Melanctha is "a Negro Madame Bovary or Esther
> Waters."

53. Cleaton, Irene and Allen. *Books and Battles: American
Literature, 1920-1930.* Boston: Houghton Mifflin, 1937.

> The last sentence of the Cleatons' sarcastic recap of Stein's
> life until 1935–titled "Miss Stein Is Idolized" (pp. 40-46)—
> reads: "And so Miss Stein, after her happy success, was laid
> away in mothballs; in all probability the only further reference
> that will be made to her is as a monumental literary curiosity
> of the nineteen-twenties."

54. Cowley, Malcolm, ed. *After the Genteel Tradition:
American Writers 1910-1930.* 1937; rpt. Carbondale:
Southern Illinois University Press, 1964.

> *After the Genteel Tradition* contains mentions of Stein in
> relation to Sherwood Anderson and Ernest Hemingway. See
> especially John Peale Bishop's contribution, "Homage to
> Hemingway" (originally in *New Republic,* 89 [11 November
> 1936], 39-42), which contains several paragraphs on Stein
> and on her influence on Hemingway. A typical article of the
> times, it notes that "her genius, unfortunately, has not yet
> arrived at the age of three years." Bishop is also critical of
> her lack of material.

55. Loggins, Vernon. *I Hear America . . . Literature in
the United States since 1900.* New York: Crowell,
1937.

> "Gertrude Stein, John Dos Passos, and Ernest Hemingway
> maintain that the sentence established according to the rules
> of rhetoric is not a unit of actual thinking and never has been.

They therefore disregard it at will. . . . But the English
language is a mighty fortress, and any attack upon it must be
minor. Even Gertrude Stein is obliged to use nouns and verbs."
Sherwood Anderson was harmed by "further ventures into
Freud and psychoanalysis and into Gertrude Stein. . . ."
Stein's theories influenced James Joyce's *Ulysses*.

The Making of Americans "is printed with a punctuation and
capitalization and sentence structure in no manner unusual.
It can be read with ease by the most custom-bound reader; it
is much less obscure than the late fiction of Henry James, upon
which it was modelled. It is one of the great twentieth-century
American novels. . . ."

Loggins incorporates biographical errors; his article on Stein
is mostly a reiteration of critical articles appearing before
1937—stressing lack of grammar, dream patterns,
monosyllables. On *The Autobiography of Alice B. Toklas*, Loggins
writes the following: "If a great new English prose is in the
making, and if Ernest Hemingway, as James Stephens thinks,
is its prime mover, then Gertrude Stein is its creator. For there
is not a stylistic device employed by Hemingway and his
numerous followers which had not been first worked out
and used by Gertrude Stein."

56. Van Ghent, Dorothy. "Gertrude Stein and the Solid
World." *American Stuff*. New York: Viking, 1937.

57. Elias, R.H. "Letters." *Story*, 10 (February 1937), 55.

58. Haas, Robert Bartlett. "Note about Gertrude Stein."
Occident, April 1937, p. 4.

59. Burnett, Whit. "Conversations with Gertrude Stein."
The Literary Life and the Hell with It. New York: Harper
and Brothers, 1939. Pp. 99-106.

In an article which first appeared in *Story* (6 [May 1935],
2), Burnett records several anecdotes and mostly column-
type chit-chat.

60. Feibleman, James. *In Praise of Comedy: A Study in*

Its Theory and Practice. London: George Allen and Unwin, 1939.

> "*Comedy, then, consists in the indirect affirmation of the ideal logical order by means of the derogation of the limited orders of actuality.*" Stein follows this principle "by confusing the categories of actuality as an indication of their ultimate unimportance, and as a warning against taking them too seriously."
>
> "Comedy . . . upsets the categories of actuality only with the purpose of affirming the logical order. The literal nonsense of Gertrude Stein calls for the establishment of wider conventions in prose than those which her own prose came to destroy." In *Tender Buttons* and *Geography and Plays*, Stein "is essentially the comedian," who "is devoted to the problem of discontinuity." Her joke is "the juxtaposition of words in sentence form, which tantalizingly sound as though they had a meaning when they have none, in an effort to ridicule meaning itself. . . ." Stein uses "a subtle variety of the comedy of meaningless . . ." and "the comedy of erroneous logical analysis."
>
> "She is a comedian in the deepest sense of the word, and this because she accomplished the opposite of what she set out to do."

61. Marine, Myra. "Being Dead Is Something." *New Republic*, 89 (20 January 1939), 365.

62. Blackmur, Richard. *The Expense of Greatness.* New York: Arrow Editions, 1940.

63. Millett, Fred B. *Contemporary American Authors: A Critical Survey and 219 Bio-Bibliographies.* London: George G. Harrap, 1940.

> "The full weight of Gertrude Stein's extraordinary influence has for years been thrown on the side of experimentation with narrative style, and her *Three Lives* (1909) . . . pointed the way to a revitalizing of style through the substitution of the rhythm and diction of speech for the rhythm and structure of literary prose, and the apparent repetitiousness and unselectivity or oral colloquial discourse for the rational selectivity of formal prose. . . ."

64. Haas, Robert Bartlett. "Note on Gertrude Stein."
    Mss., 1940, p. 4.

65. Wilcox, Wendell. "A Note on Stein and Abstraction."
    Poetry, 55 (February 1940), 254-57.

    Wilcox's article relates to "Stanzas in Meditation I-VI"
    printed in this issue. He seems to have read William Troy
    (II-E-xi-7), and then attempted to enlarge upon it; Wilcox is
    also interested in Stein's "destiny" of abstract writing.

    "In much of her prose you meet recurrence to and calling
    and recalling upon a single person or thing, and the prose
    style which she has invented for her use, being patterned and
    rhythmic not in the sense of set patterns and meters, but in
    the sense of the play and movement between the words
    themselves, has in it a tone and quality which comes close
    to poetry."

66. Cargill, Oscar. *Intellectual America: Ideas on the March.*
    New York: Macmillan, 1941.

    "In place of the scissors and newspaper of Tzara, these
    mystifiers" (a "super-realist group" headed by André Breton
    and influenced by Gertrude Stein) "have substituted
    automatic writing."

    Stein's predominant influence was on e. e. cummings.

    There are many mentions—of influences, relationships,
    and so on—especially in "The Decadents," pp. 293-99, and
    "The Primitivists," pp. 311-28. Cargill has interesting
    interpretations of the influences on Stein; she moved from
    Decadence to synesthesia and thus to automatism. "*Tender
    Buttons* is really a series of Cubist pictures in words. In theory,
    they are poems in which the meaning of the word is entirely
    self-contained and does not depend upon external
    reference. It is an effort to discover intrinsic values in
    words—to disregard words as symbols or signs. As a scientific
    experiment *Tender Buttons* is an interesting failure; as art
    the book is a preposterous joke which, since it failed, its author
    has had to take seriously." "*Tender Buttons* is a failure as a
    scientific experiment because Miss Stein has no perfect
    criteria for distinguishing the automatic from the conscious
    creation; because, without separating them, she has printed
    the two together"; Cargill then discusses "A Red Stamp."

He criticizes Stein for her egocentricity, and also criticizes
B.F. Skinner who, in writing of Stein's automatism, "has
postponed, rather than hastened, the general comprehension
of Miss Stein's work. For automatism is after all a means and
not an end; it is a technique and not a purpose; Mr. Skinner
has shown us nothing at all about Gertrude Stein's intentions."

Intellectual America contains an interesting discussion of the
inception of Stein's work, and includes a discussion of
"Melanctha," which begins on p. 314:

In the telling of "Melanctha" Miss Stein was as original
as in choosing her materials. She foresaw that she must
make the tale as simple in statement as it was in its
substance. There must be nothing in it which would not be
naturally phrased in the mind of Melanctha herself had she
dramatized her own story. It must contain the phrases she
would repeat if she were thus constantly dramatizing it.
This is accomplished by restricting the vocabulary . . . and
by repeating certain descriptive phrases which characterize
the types of people found in the tale. There is no automatic
writing in "Melanctha"; there is, however, exploited what
Miss Stein had learned in her experiment in Cambridge and
by reading Galton. . . .

The student of literature, familiar with the now discarded
theory of ballad origins, will say that the tale of "Melanctha"
is built up by "incremental repetition," and just as this
device heightens the effect of the ballad, so it improves this
tale. When the originality of the material, the ingenuity of
the telling, and the effect desired by the author are all taken
into account, it is hard to see how this piece could be
improved. Both for historical reasons and for intrinsic merit,
"Melanctha" must be ranked as one of the three or four
thoroughly original short stories which have been produced
in this century.

67. Gold, Michael. *The Hollow Men*. New York:
International Publishers, 1941.

"*The Hollow Men* appeared originally as a series of articles
in the Daily Worker under the title 'The Great Tradition: Can
the Literary Renegades Destroy It?' " Stein receives some
mentions throughout an interpretation of literary history.

68. Murdoch, Walter. *Collected Essays of Walter Murdoch.* London: Angus and Robertson, 1941.

   The main essay in which Murdoch writes about Stein is "Nihilism in Literature" (pp. 218-22), mainly a criticism of "Elucidation." James Joyce and Miss Stein are "silly."

69. Levinson, Ronald. "Gertrude Stein, William James, and Grammar." *American Journal of Psychology,* 54 (January 1941), 124-28.

   In an attempt to modify B.F. Skinner's "automatic writing" claim, Levinson writes that "ours is the far easier objective of suggesting, from the point of view of Miss Stein's interest in language, and her theory of its use, a definite purpose underlying her radical breach with the grammar of her native tongue." Levinson takes "into the reckoning certain quite definitive stylistic doctrines of Miss Stein's which are on the conscious levels of her mind. . . ." The writings that do approach automatic writing are attempts "to put into practice some notions of the ideal functions of language, notions which were in all probability derived from . . . William James."

70. Brooks, Van Wyck. *Opinions of Oliver Allston.* London: Dent, 1942.

   Allston/Brooks considers Marcel Proust, Paul Valéry and Stein secondary (as opposed to primary) writers because they wrote "coterie literature"; they denied progress, and doubted "the value of life and of literature also." In Stein's case, after *Three Lives,* this was partially due to living in a country not her own and writing for a society which "has no associations in common. The uprooted world of cosmopolitan urban people can meet only on the plane of abstractions."

71. Kallen, Horace M. *Art and Freedom: A Historical and Biographical Interpretation of the Relations between the Ideas of Beauty, Use and Freedom in Western Civilization from the Greeks to the Present Day,* II. New York: Duell, Sloan and Pearce, 1942.

   In Chapter 26, "The Visual Contamination of the Verbal Arts," Section 113 appears "The Imagists: Gertrude Stein." *Tender Buttons* is "a mutation upon the Imagist practice."

72. Schlauch, Margaret. *The Gift of Tongues*. New York: Modern Age Books, 1942.

> *Gift of Tongues* is a linguistics book for "the educated reader with an unprofessional, merely casual interest in language."
> Schlauch is mostly concerned with *Ida* and *Four Saints in Three Acts.* "Her consciously primitivistic vocabulary—a very different thing, by the way, from a primitive one!—is a perpetual challenge to the reader to create afresh the intended abstractions out of presented monosyllables." Schlauch makes a considerable attempt to explicate parts of *Four Saints* and "Florence Descotes." "Much of the Steinian text is constructed for sound alone, and there is also much jocosity in the form of puns, bizarre juxtapositions, and startling transitions. . . ."
> ". . . the rather snobbish pleasure derived from collaborating with [Stein] in a quest for meaning is not great enough to justify the effort and the slight results. . . . To a lesser degree than Joyce she does provide a kind of linguistic rejuvenation by a method of her own, but other poets give a heightened pleasure in language with far less sacrifice of propositional content."

73. Pearson, N.H. "Gertrude Stein Collection." *Yale University Library Gazette*, 16 (January 1942), 45-47.

> Pearson's article concerns the Yale exhibition in 1941. See I-A-i-4.

74. Haines, George, IV. "Forms of Imaginative Prose: 1900-1940." *Southern Review*, 7 (Spring 1942), 755-75.

> Gertrude Stein is discussed between pp. 766 and 769.
> ". . . literature, because it is an art employing language as a medium, may be either predominantly 'semantic' or predominantly 'iconic' . . . the novelist may present his perception using language as *reference* to the reality or may present his perception using language as *imitation* of reality." Gertrude Stein uses language imitatively. Haines discusses Stein's use of words to imitate individuality; repetition and patterns are the key to the identification of reality. He also refers to *Three Lives, Making of Americans*, and *If I Told Him* (in which Haines uses theme and variation to describe what occurs).

75. Sawyer, Julian. "Wilder and Stein: The Kinship between *Our Town* and *The Making of Americans*." *Saturday Review*, 17 April 1943, p. 27. Compiler is unable to verify the existence of this article.

76. Cowley, Malcolm. "The Middle American Style: D. Crockett to E. Hemingway." *New York Times*, 15 July 1945, Sec. 7, p. 3.

   Cowley emphasizes Ernest Hemingway in his article, but traces the development of his, and Stein's, style to the nineteenth century and attempts to capture dialects in print. See also Richard Bridgman's *Colloquial Style*, II-C-151.

77. Desfeuilles, P. (Paul). *Une Fervente de la répétition: Gertrude Stein*. Mirefleurs, 1946.

   "Gertrude Stein, dont la disparition vient d'endeuiller les Letres, présent, comme un polyèdre, de multiples facettes. Tour à tour romancière, poëtesse, conférencière, grammairienne, philosophe, memorialiste, journaliste, critique d'art, cette Américaine nous étonne par l'universalité de son génie."
   What follows these opening sentences is a monograph on Stein and her work. Desfeuilles includes many examples of her work, in French. He also discusses the American language and how it is differentiated from British English, and Stein's repetition.
   See also "La grammaire et la poësie, d'après Gertrude Stein." Yggdrasill, 25 October 1937, pp. 115-17. Of lesser importance is "Au fil de la littérature: Gertrude Stein et le 'Vrai Present'." *Le Bayou* (University of Houston), 40 (Winter 1949), 31-39.

78. Brodin, Pierre. "Gertrude Stein," in *Les Écrivains américains du vingtième siècle*. Paris: Horizons de France, 1947. Pp. 25-44.

   A general article of Stein and her writing.

79. Burgum, Edwin Berry. "The Genius of Miss Gertrude
Stein." *The Novel and the World's Dilemma*. New York:
Oxford University Press, 1947. Pp. 157-83.

> Burgum discusses *Three Lives, Making of Americans, Portraits and
> Prayers,* and *Four Saints.* His is a strange psychological, social,
> literary and historical approach to the whole problem of Stein,
> and the chapter is not without biographical errors.
> Her writing, the use of "a new American language," "can be
> traced back to the pioneer work of Mark Twain."

80. Canby, Henry Seidel. *American Memoir*. Boston:
Houghton Mifflin, 1947.

> In his reappraisal of Stein, Canby remarks that "hers was a
> one-woman revolt against the dominance of rhythms over the
> word itself, which had lost its suggestive quality by being fitted
> into a standardized syntax or a required grammatical form. . . .
> She forced the attention . . . to the peculiar feeling and
> suggestions of the words themselves. . . . Yet I still cannot
> read her without losing my temper."

81. Gagey, Edmond M. *Revolution in American Drama*. New
York: Columbia University Press, 1947.

> Stein's *Four Saints in Three Acts* approximates "the ideals of
> [Gordon] Craig [*The Art of the Theatre* (1905), *On the Art of the
> Theatre* (1911)]—purely aesthetic drama, divorced from realism,
> depending for its effects upon a fusion of the arts."

82. Evans, Oliver. "Gertrude Stein As Humorist." *Prairie
Schooner*, 21 (Spring 1947), 97-102.

> Stein was one of America's "greatest humorists," and her
> humor was "characteristically American—and frontier American
> at that." Despite some errors and false implications, Evans's is
> a very interesting discussion of Stein's humor, which "functions
> most consistently and delightfully" perhaps in her
> "autobiographical works."

83. Gallup, Donald. "The Gertrude Stein Collection."
Yale University Library Gazette, 22 (October 1947), 22-32.

84. Gloster, Hugh M. *Negro Voices in American Fiction.* Chapel Hill: University of North Carolina Press, 1948.

Gertrude Stein "was likewise a sponsor of the African Art Movement" (as author of "Melanctha"). "Another stimulus to the cultural interest of the American Negro in Africa derived from the rediscovery of primitive African painting and sculpture by French artists during the first quarter of the present century."

Gloster mentions "Melanctha" several times. Stein and others "made departures from the stereotyped presentation of colored characters."

85. Young, Stark. *Immortal Shadows: A Book of Dramatic Criticism.* New York: Scribner's Sons, 1948.

Young includes *"Four Saints in Three Acts,"* pp. 150-52, "the most important event of the theatre season. . . . It is the first free, pure theatre that I have seen so far." "The spring and melodic fantasy of the music, the scenario, the choreography and the décor arise quite profoundly and organically from the piece Miss Stein has written. . . . The actual words themselves . . . are a secondary part of it."

86. Gallup, Donald. "A Book Is a Book Is a Book." *New Colophon,* 1 (January 1948), 67-80.

Gallup here researches the history of Stein's first publication, *Three Lives.* Included are prepublication criticisms by both publishing companies and friends.

87. Evans, Oliver. "The Americanism of Gertrude Stein." *Prairie Schooner,* 22 (Spring 1948), 70-74.

"When one considers the range of the late Gertrude Stein's published writings . . . , one is immediately impressed by the fact that they reveal a sensibility which is profoundly and uniquely American": "the attitudes . . . the humor . . . even the very accents and cadences of the language. . . ."

88. Anderson, George K. and Edna Lou Walton. *This Generation: A Selection of British and American Literature*

from 1914 to the Present. Rev. ed. Chicago: Scott, Foresman, 1949.

Stein is treated as one of the stream-of-consciousness pioneers. Anderson and Walton mix truth, exaggeration, and error in an insistent attempt to make Stein appear as a great experimenter with a cause: "Her attack upon the mediocrity of the middle-class consciousness was in fact an attack upon the typical middle-class use of language. By the use of words out of context, by destroying the typical sentence syntax, she satirized other literary forms as too conventional and the conventional literary emotions as trite. . . . She was of course one of the chief figures among that group of artists, of whom Cummings was also one, who saw in the break-up of institutionalized forms of expression the possibility of expressing the artist's peculiar sensitivity."

This Generation contains part of *Four Saints in Three Acts*, "Miss Furr and Miss Skeene," and "Ada."

89. Gallup, Donald. "Always Gtrde Stein." *Southwest Review*, 34 (Summer 1949), 254-58.

Printed here are ten previously unpublished letters from Stein to Gallup—plus personal commentary by Gallup—between 1941 and 1946.

90. Haines, George, IV. "Gertrude Stein and Composition." *Sewanee Review*, 57 (Summer 1949), 411-24.

Stein is a "seminal writer."

In showing the evolution of Stein's work, Haines discusses *Making of Americans, Long Gay Book, The Geographical History of America,* "Lipschitz," and *Brewsie and Willie.* Haines also points out the proximity of Stein's prose to poetry. The author is always present in Stein's work. In *Long Gay Book,* Stein turned from strict autobiography to the immediate experience.

91. Ernest, Gifford. "Reader Be Damned." *Saturday Review*, 33 (27 May 1950), 23-24.

A *Letter(s) to the Editor* in response to "They Think They Know Joyce" by Oliver St-John Gogarty (*Saturday Review*, 18 March

1950, pp. 8-9 and 35-37), this article comes to the same conclusion as Gogarty's, "that in art—all art—there should be nothing obscure or incomprehensible."

92. Braddy, Haldeen. "The Primitive in Gertrude Stein's 'Melanctha'." *New Mexico Quarterly*, 20 (Autumn 1950), 358-65.

93. Gallup, Donald. "The Making of *The Making of Americans*." *New Colophon*, 3 (1950), 54-74.

   This history of the composition and publication of *The Making of Americans* is reprinted in *Fernhurst, Q.E.D., and Other Early Writings*.

94. Janzon, Åke. "Gertrude Stein." *Bonniers Litterära Magasin*, 7 (September 1950), 528-31.

95. Bogan, Louise. *Achievement in American Poetry 1900-1950*. Chicago: Henry Regnery, 1951.

   "It is interesting to note that 1914 was the year of the publication of James Joyce's *Dubliners*, stories in which Joyce was still definitely tied to the more formal nineteenth-century French tradition of fiction. Therefore, Miss Stein's experiments, in which logical meaning is definitely eliminated, are the first of the kind to reach America and to be caught up by the poetic experimentalists who were then functioning."
   Bogan also mentions *Tender Buttons*, "a small collection of poems," *Three Lives* ("the new direction in which creative and critical winds were blowing") and Stein's portraits.

96. Cowley, Malcolm. *Exile's Return: A Literary Odyssey of the 1920's*. London: The Bodley Head, 1951.

   Exile's Return contains several small Stein mentions, mostly anecdotal. Cowley seems to set up Stein as a literary movement with Functionalism and Surrealism.

97. Straumann, Heinrich. *American Literature in the Twentieth Century*. London: Hutchinson's University Library, 1951.

   "A considerable part of [Stein's] experimental writing

appears merely to consist of practical exercises in application
of the theory. . . ." *Three Lives*, which "already contains all the
essential characteristics of Gertrude Stein, but without its
later excrescences and mannerisms," will perhaps be her only
book "read for its own sake."

The difficulty of giving an adequate rendering of the
consciousness and the mood of such people [Anna, Lena,
and Melanctha, "less articulate than that of a fully educated
person"] is met by Gertrude Stein's method as hardly ever
before. Here the extreme plainness of the vocabulary and the
use of repetition as means to emphasize the living moment
appear entirely to the point. At the same time the objectivity
of the artist is so absolute that one cannot decide whether she
takes sides with any of the values that her heroines believe in.
Though this remoteness of intention, together with the
mannerism of her later work, may well account for a decrease
of Gertrude Stein's fame as a writer, her influence on the
technique of the whole "lost generation" can hardly be
overrated. After all, it was she who discovered the secret
of subtlety through utmost simplicity in the smaller units of
speech.

98. Whicher, George F. "Gertrude Stein and Her
Experimental Techniques," in *The Literature of the
American People: An Historical and Critical Survey.* Ed.
Arthur Hobson Quinn. New York: Appleton-Century-
Crofts, 1951. Pp. 864-66.

    The Autobiography of Alice B. Toklas is "the best approach to the
writings of Gertrude Stein." *Wars I Have Seen* "will certainly
remain one of the great documents inspired by the Second
World War." "Miss Stein's experimentalism was rooted in her
own first-hand knowledge of psychology, not in a thin dilution
of Freud."

99. McBride, Henry. "Pictures for a Picture of Gertrude."
Art News, 49 (February 1951), 16-18 and 63.

    McBride's is a review of the Yale University Art Gallery show
and a memoir. He had visited Gertrude and Alice "in 1912 or
1913." McBride writes that the bell rang "in AliceToklas'
bosom." (Alice B. Toklas met three geniuses in her lifetime,
and each time a bell rang.)

100. Brooks, Van Wyck. *The Confident Years: 1885-1915.*
New York: Dutton, 1952.

> Brooks mentions Stein and her works on many different
> occasions, especially pp. 254-60 and 334-46. "Melanctha"—
> in fact all of *Three Lives*—proved that Stein "was a true
> creator."
> While Stein wrote of things that interested her, "that stirred
> her emotionally," her work was very good and at times very
> perceptive; "when she began to 'write cubistically' . . . she
> dispensed with the subject that had stirred her and focused her
> mind. So her writing became a chaos of words and rhythms. . . ."

101. Pivano, Fernanda. "Gertrude Stein, pioniera di un
secolo." *Pensiero Critico* (Milano), No. 5 (March 1952).

102. Gallup, Donald. "Carl Van Vechten's Gertrude
Stein." *Yale University Library Gazette,* 27 (October
1952), 77-86.

> The friendship (and, essential to that, correspondences) of
> Van Vechten and Stein—the relationship of two people
> important to twentieth-century American letters—is discussed
> in this article.

103. Reid, Benjamin. "Gertrude Stein's Critics."
University of Kansas City Review, 19 (Winter 1952),
121-30.

> Reprinted in *Art by Subtraction* (II-A-12), this article is a look
> at Stein criticism up to 1952; it is only slightly updated for
> inclusion in the book through two references, actually only a
> listing, to Elizabeth Sprigge's 1957 biography (I-B-i-16). There
> are two extremes: "First, [at] the hyperbolic schools of
> adoration and vilification; then a longer look at the soberer
> judgments, concentrating particularly on the essays of Edmund
> Wilson and Thornton Wilder." Stein criticism is "not
> particularly interesting. It is startlingly small, very generally
> mistaken, undernourished in fact, usually unbalanced in
> illogical admiration or in illogical peevishness,
> characteristically low in specific gravity."

104. Burman, Ben Lucien. "Cult of Unintelligibility."
Saturday Review, 35 (1 November 1952), 9-10 and 38.
Discussion of article follows in *Saturday Review*, 35
(29 November 1952), 23-24.

Burman declares that Stein and the later James Joyce are
lacking in talent. The high point of this article is a literary game:
eight quotations are given, and the reader is to identify the
author; the choices are Joyce, Stein, or a mentally-ill/brain-
damaged patient.

The letters from Lawrence A. Wiggin and Frank S. MacShane
in 29 November *Saturday Review* are proof of more objective and
honest attempts to approach both Stein's and Joyce's works.

105. Brooks, Van Wyck. *The Writer in America*. New York:
Dutton, 1953.

Brooks mentions Stein several times as "an astute observer"
and "highly intuitive."

106. Tate, Allen. *Sixty American Poets 1896-1944*.
Washington: Library of Congress, 1954.

107. Gallup, Donald. "Gertrude Stein and the *Atlantic*."
Yale University Library Gazette, 28 (January 1954),
109-28.

This concerns, and prints, the correspondence between
Gertrude Stein and Ellery Sedgwick, editor of *Atlantic Monthly*.

108. Las Vergnas, Raymond. "Lettres anglo-américaines:
Gertrude Stein." *Hommes et Mondes*, 9 (September
1954), 315.

109. Garvin, Harry Raphael. "Sound and Sense in *Four
Saints in Three Acts*." *Bucknell Review*, 5 (December
1954), 1-11.

Garvin's is an explication of *Four Saints*, directed towards a
critical evaluation of Stein as an artist. See Richard Bridgman,
Gertrude Stein in Pieces, p. 179 (II-A-2), for his appraisal of
Garvin's essay.

Four Saints in Three Acts is "an original creation with significant

themes and characters—a masterly achievement of a major
stylist." Also, "her most revolutionary innovation" was "her
'portrait' style." Garvin distinguishes between four different
types of portrait: "of persons and objects"; "portrait-plays";
"portrait-operas"; and "portrait-novels." "In these genres,
she presented herself with radical literary problems for which
she invented radical linguistic and stylistic solutions."

In order to explicate Stein's "more mature portrait
compositions," "the reader . . . must study each scene and
act in relation to the whole, must watch for recurring symbols,
and must discover the dominant feeling and idea of each
scene."

In *Four Saints* Stein seldom "permits sound to triumph over
sense; there are only a few purely mellifluous passages. Only
occasionally does she indulge in rhymes and seducing sounds
that complicate the meaning unnecessarily. . . . The main
purpose of the puns, the nursery rhymes, the quick
buffoonery, and the playful comments . . . is . . . to
remind the reader that warmer, subtler kinds of humor
and gaiety suffuse the whole of *Four Saints*. . . ." Repetition
affects "the meaning and are [sic] apropos to the sense and the
sound in this opera."

Garvin's is an interesting albeit sometimes simplistic
appraisal of *Four Saints in Three Acts,* and of Stein's method
of creation.

110. Cowley, Malcolm. *The Literary Situation.* New York:
Viking, 1955.

"The creation of a rich and flexible prose style based on
Midwestern rather than New England speech . . . as a literary
medium . . . derives from Mark Twain . . . but it also owes a
great deal to Gertrude Stein and Sherwood Anderson."

111. Sievers, W. David. *Freud on Broadway: A History of
Psychoanalysis and the American Drama.* New York:
Hermitage House, 1955.

This is mainly a book on drama that has derived its themes
from psychoanalysis. There is a short section on Stein.

"Of all the playwrights, the one who apparently set out to
suppress the conscious as rigidly as the pre-Freudians suppressed
the unconscious was Gertrude Stein. . . ." Sievers makes the

comparison between Bach's contrapuntal fugues and Stein's writings several times. He is most concerned with *Yes Is for a Very Young Man.*

"Miss Stein was disassociated from the mainstream of drama, and there are those who believe that she was only playing a great joke on the gullible public, conditioned by Freudianism to accept the irrational and incoherent, afraid to be called 'old-fashioned' by rejecting it but deriving from it neither aesthetic benefit nor psychiatric benefit."

112. Spiller, Robert E. *The Cycle of American Literature: An Essay in Historical Criticism.* New York: Free Press, 1955.

Stein's discovery was "that art could live in 'the complete actual present' by using words out of formal context as the plastic elements of direct expression." Also important was her "concern for the primitive consciousness."

113. Untermeyer, Louis. *Makers of the Modern World.* New York: Simon and Schuster, 1955.

114. Heissenbüttel, Helmut. "Reduzierte Sprache. Über ein Stück von Gertrude Stein." *Augenblick,* 1 January 1955. Pp. 1-16.

"Sich mit [Steins] Werk beschäftigen heisst zuerst und vor allem, die Kategorie des Inhaltlichen fallenzulassen." Section one is one of the best short introductions to Stein's work; the second section consists of "As a Wife Has a Cow. A Love Story"; section three is an analysis of the second section. Heissenbüttel examines "As a Wife Has a Cow" from literary and linguistic bases.

115. Garvin, Harry Raphael. "Stein's 'Lipschitz'." *Explicator,* 14 (December 1955), No. 18.

116. Cambon, Glauco. *Tematica e Sviluppo della Poesia Americana.* Rome: Edizioni di Storia e Letteratura, 1956.

This edition contains two more references to Stein—once to her "audacia sperimentali"—than the later, translated edition.

117. Foster, Jeannette. *Sex Variant Women in Literature.* 2nd
ed. 1956; Baltimore, Maryland: Diana Press, 1975.

Foster discusses *Things As They Are*, pp. 247-51. On p. 334
Anaïs Nin is described as "a stylistic disciple (in some measure)
of Gertrude Stein."

118. Blöcker, Günter. "Die Muse der verlorenen
Generation." *Merkur*, 10 (July 1956), 720-24.
Reprinted in Günter Blöcker, *Die neuen Wirklichkeiten:
Linien und Profile der modernen Literatur.* Berlin: Argon
Verlag, 1957. Pp. 232-40.

Stein was the mother or the midwife of the modern American
novel. "Die meisten ihrer Arbeiten sind mehr Tabellenwerk
und ästhetisches Beweismaterial als eigentliche
Kunstleistungen. . . . Ihre eigene Vitalität aber (und die
war beträchtlich) verausgabte sich in der Wollust des
Experiments, in der literarischen Bastelei." Stein recognized
that F. Scott Fitzgerald, not Ernest Hemingway, was "das Genie
der 'verlorenen Generation'."

"Dennoch bleibt die Tatsache, dass Gertrude Stein vor allem
in Hemingway und seinen stilistischen Errungenschaften
fortlebt: in seinem Lakonismus, seiner erarbeiteten
Objektivität, seinem konstatierenden Verhältnis zur
Wirklichkeit, seinem kunstvollen Primitivismus; besonders
aber in seiner Technik, nicht Empfindungen zu beschreiben,
sondern durch rhythmische Abläufe Empfindungen zu erzeugen,
dem Leser durch exakte Wiedergabe der Oberfläche
Innenansichten (*'insides'*) zu vermitteln. Was die Welt von
Gertrude Stein kennt, kennt sie durch Hemingway, auch wenn
sie nichts davon weiss. . . ."

The article is written on the occasion of the first German
translation of one of Stein's works, *The Autobiography of Alice
B. Toklas.*

119. Bense, Max. "Kosmologie und Literatur: Über
Alfred N. Whitehead und Gertrude Stein." *Texte
und Zeichen*, 3 (1957), 512-25.

120. Clurman, Harold. *Lies Like Truth: Theatre Reviews and Essays*. New York: Macmillan, 1958.

The article "Stein and O'Casey" (1953) reviews the stage production of *Brewsie and Willie* by Ellen Violett and Liz Blake.

121. Walther, Elisabeth. "Notizen über Gertrude Stein." *Augenblick*, 3 (3 January 1958), 45-51.

122. Gass, William H. "Gertrude Stein: Her Escape from Protective Language." *Accent*, 18 (Autumn 1958), 233-44.

Gass's article is based on disagreement with Benjamin Reid's *Art by Subtraction* (II-A-12), which is "a muddled and angry piece of journalese whose only value lies in how well it expresses the normal academic reaction and how superbly it contains and how characteristically it uses those malicious inferences fear lends so readily to anger." Prodded, perhaps, by Reid's misconceptions of Stein's literary theories and misreadings of both theoretical and creative works, Gass examines her use of "protective language," her experimentation, her theories and their worth. Her writings, from the very beginning, challenged literary criticism. This challenge "asks for nothing less than a study of the entire basis of our criticism" and "requires us to consider again the esthetic significance of style; to examine again the ontological status of the artist's vision, his medium, and his effect. None of the literary innovators who were her contemporaries attempted anything like the revolution she proposed, and because her methods were so uncompromising, her work cannot really be met except on the finest and most fundamental grounds."

"Art is not a form of simple communication."

123. Baldanza, Frank. "Faulkner and Stein: A Study in Stylistic Intransigence." *Georgia Review*, 13 (Fall 1959), 274-86.

Mr. Baldanza discusses and compares William Faulkner's *Absalom, Absalom!* and Stein's *The Making of Americans*.

124. Howard, Leon. *Literature and the American Tradition*.
New York: Doubleday, 1960.

Stein is "one of the most historically important writers of her
time."

125. Ashton, Dore. "Writing and Painting: A Parallel."
New York Times, 31 January 1960, Sec. 2, p. 17.

Gertrude Stein is "perhaps the only writer in history who took
the principles of painting literally and applied them to the word
—or at least she was the only one who said she did, and did."

126. Hassan, Ihab H. "Love in the Modern American
Novel: Expense of Spirit and Waste of Shame."
Western Humanities Review, 14 (Spring 1960),
149-61.

In section 2, p. 153, Hassan writes: "Stein had written in
'Melanctha', 1909, as perfect a love story as America had seen,
though few Americans were in the mood then to follow the
painful poetry, the endless beginnings, the slow knotting and
unknotting of love in that work. . . ."

127. Pivano, Fernanda. "Il soggiorno romano de Alice B.
Toklas." *L'Europa Letteraria*, 2 (February 1961), 100-05.

128. Corke, Hilary. "Reflections on a Great Stone Face."
Kenyon Review, 23 (Summer 1961), 367-89.

In the first part of the article, which is concerned with Stein's
Stanzas in Meditation and Elizabeth Sprigge's *Gertrude Stein*
(I-B-i-16), Corke struggles to discover or uncover a method in
Stein's madness. He feels he has, "on the whole, done the best
for Gertrude that [he] honestly could." And, aside from a
tendency to scoff, Corke effectively and intuitively sounds out
the problems (for the majority of readers) present in *Stanzas
in Meditation* and in Donald Sutherland's introduction (II-D-15).
Corke also brings up questions which, by the 1960s, were
already very trite: why did Yale publish Stein; why did
Sutherland write an introduction. He also refers to the "mass
hallucination" responsible for Stein's success, and to Stein
hitching her reputation to Pablo Picasso's "so that they rose
together."

129. Bridgman, Richard. " 'Melanctha'." *American Literature*, 33 (November 1961), 350-59.

Bridgman notes that " 'Melanctha' is a full-scale reworking of Gertrude Stein's first book, *Things As They Are* . . . ," which Leo Stein had previously noted. Bridgman seems to be the first critic to take Leo Stein's comments seriously and to apply them to "Melanctha." The first section of Bridgman's article is concerned with the similarities between the two works; the remainder is a discussion of "Melanctha," including the sexuality and the style of the work. The prose is "erratic, uneven, and tedious," perhaps because "Stein tried to conceal her subject in swirls of verbal obscurity."

130. Hoffman, Frederick J. *The Twenties: American Writing in the Postwar Decade.* New York: Viking, 1962.

There are many mentions of Stein (and a discussion of *Making of Americans*); the main discussion occurs in Chapter 5, "Forms of Experiment and Improvisation," Section 3, "The Color and Shape of the Thing Seen: Gertrude Stein." Her significant contributions were a sense of the immediate present and a fully documented discussion of the aesthetic strategies required to make immediacy functional within a prose text." Hoffman also acknowledges Stein's influence on Ernest Hemingway.

131. Spiller, Robert E., ed. *A Time of Harvest: American Literature 1910-1960.* New York: Hill and Wang, 1962.

Stein is particularly discussed in "Poetry and Language," by Norman Holmes Pearson. "When Gertrude Stein strives for the achievement of a constant present in her prose she is representing by the structuring of her text what [Henri] Bergson and [Alfred North] Whitehead were asserting philosophically in regard to the now-ness of time. In following the new advances of experimental psychology as she had learned them at Radcliffe College under William James, she was exploring a new field of realism in which we know man not by description but by what he does: character is not to be conceived of in ethical terms but in individualities."

132. Weales, Gerald. *American Drama Since World War II*.
New York: Harcourt, Brace and World, 1962.

Weales discusses the adaptation by Ellen Violett and Lisbeth
Blake of *Brewsie and Willie* for off-Broadway (1953). Stein imitates
the "aimlessness and earnestness of GI talk" through "her use of
repetition and interruption."

133. Beaver, Howard. "A Figure in the Carpet: Irony and
the American Novel." *Essays and Studies*, 15 (1962),
101-14.

"Gertrude Stein, in her muddled way, did see the problem"
[in the novel]: "an inflated verbiage . . . which had lost touch
not only with [their] own speaking voice but with the English
of its supposed origin."

Beaver's chronology is wrong. His judgment of Stein is that
her style "too often . . . grew trite, repetitious, naïve."

134. Kesting, Marianne. "Gertrude Stein: Das
Experiment des Experiments." *Panorama des
zeitgenössischen Theaters: 50 literarische Porträts*.
München: R. Piper, 1962. Pp. 43-49.

Kesting's article contains much false information. At the very
beginning she attempts to present Stein's mini-biography in six
sentences; this leads to many misrepresentations. Kesting writes,
for instance, that Stein was "ab 1902 in Europa (Paris)." This
mini-biography is immediately followed with a chronological
listing of "Dramen," which contains many errors—both in titles
and in dates. Kesting's discussion of Stein's dramas includes the
same paragraph from "Gradual Making of *The Making of
Americans*" as a later article; this, her earlier translation, is as
inaccurate as—although differing slightly from—the later.

135. Haas, Robert Bartlett. "Gertrude Stein Talking—A
Transatlantic Interview." *Uclan Review*, 8 (Summer 1962),
3-11; 9 (Spring 1963), 40-48; 9 (Winter 1964), 44-48.

This is excerpted in *A Primer for the Gradual Understanding
of Gertrude Stein*, ed. Robert Bartlett Haas (Los Angeles:
Black Sparrow Press, 1971).

136. Kesting, Marianne. "Gertrude Steins dramatische Versuche." *Neue Deutsche Hefte,* 88 (July-August 1962), 10:

137. Deutsch, Babette. *Poetry in Our Times: A Critical Survey of Poe* in *the English-Speaking World 1900-1960.* New York: Double (Anchor Books), 1963.

> The section on Stein is a summary of what was written in *This Modern Poetry* (II-C-38).

138. Spiller, Robert E., et al. *Literary History of the United States.* New York: Macmillan, 1963.

139. Wright, G. T. "Gertrude Stein and Her Ethic of Self-Containment." *Tennessee Studies in Literature,* 8 (1963), 17-23.

140. Huebsch, B. W. "From a Publisher's Commonplace Book." *American Scholar,* 33 (Winter 1963-64), 116 and 118.

> In Autumn 1911 Heubsch received Stein's *Making of Americans,* and this is his version of the story Donald Gallup had referred to in his *Colophon* article. The article contains letters of recommendation from Louise Collier Wilcox, who had refused Stein for Macmillan.

141. Takuwa, Shinji. "The Method of Stein's *Three Lives."* *Eigo Eibungakiu Ronso,* 14 (January 1964), 127-38.

142. Berthoff, Warner. *The Ferment of Realism: American Literature, 1884-1919.* New York: Free Press, 1965.

> In Chapter 4, "Lives of the Americans: The Class of the '70s," "Jack London, Gertrude Stein" appears (pp. 244-53). The six pages or so on Stein are insubstantial. Berthoff discusses *Making of Americans* and *Three Lives.* Her "development as a writer of fiction was wholly technical." He feels her "later critical papers" will be the most lasting of her works. "Potentially a comic writer of genuine force and point, Gertrude Stein is unable to grasp the major traditional occasions of prose comedy, which have to do with human behavior as shaped not only by the biological and

perceptual rhythms she was preoccupied with but also by economic obligation, in the broadest sense, and by the social contract, which she ignored."

143.   Cambon, Glauco. *The Inclusive Flame: Studies in Modern American Poetry.* Bloomington: Indiana University Press, 1965.

Cambon refers to Stein twice, once to her "furiously wrenching sound from meaning through obsessive repetition, as if words were some kind of fissionable material to be bombarded in a cyclotron."

144. Spiller, Robert E. *The Third Dimension: Studies in Literary History.* New York: Macmillan, 1965.

145. Tanner, Tony. "Gertrude Stein and the Complete Actual Present," in *The Reign of Wonder: Naivety and Reality in American Literature.* Cambridge: Cambridge University Press, 1965. Pp. 187-204.

Tanner, like Richard Bridgman in *The Colloquial Style* (II-C-151) is interested in the development of the "vernacular narrator" from Mark Twain to Ernest Hemingway. Stein was the "indispensable provoking theorist." Tanner says that, although Stein's works are not now appreciated, "it should be pointed out that she had an unusually penetrating insight into the intellectual climate of her time and a gift for the clarification of ideas and novel experiment." Tanner is interested in Stein as an innovator, and attempts to locate "those of her ideas which might have been seminal. . . ." It is through the examination of her literary theories that one is enabled to see why she was unable to write a work that strictly followed those theories.

146. Tallman, Warren. "The Writing Life." *New American Story.* Ed. Donald M. Allen and Robert Creeley. New York: Grove Press, 1965.

William Carlos Williams and Gertrude Stein are "battler(s) for a new American writing." See especially the first section of this piece.

147. Hoffman, Michael J. "Gertrude Stein in the Psychology Laboratory." *American Quarterly*, 17 (Spring 1965), 127-32.

This is reprinted in *Development of Abstractionism* (II-A-7). Hoffman traces the development of Stein's psychological theories.

148. Thomson, Virgil. "About Four Saints." *American Record Guide*, 31 (February 1965), 520-21.

149. Hoffman, Michael J. "Gertrude Stein's 'Portraits'." *Twentieth-Century Literature*, 11 (October 1965), 115-22.

This appears to be part of the discussion on "Portraits" taken from Chapter 5, "Portraits and the Abstract Style, 1908-1912," *Development of Abstractionism* (II-A-7).

150. Anderson, Peter S. "Gertrude Stein's *Tender Buttons*: Two Rosaries." *Poet and Critic*, 1 (Winter 1965), 32-42.

151. Bridgman, Richard. "Gertrude Stein." *The Colloquial Style in America*. New York: Oxford University Press, 1966. Pp. 165-94.

Bridgman discusses Stein's works—in particular *Tender Buttons, Q.E.D.*, "Melanctha," and *Making of Americans*—as related to that of other "stylistic experimenters," Mark Twain, Henry James, Sherwood Anderson, Ring Lardner, and Ernest Hemingway.

"Her important technical contributions were made by 1914 when *Tender Buttons* was written."

152. Hoffman, Michael J. "Gertrude Stein and William James." *Personalist*, 47 (Spring 1966), 226-33.

This piece was originally printed as Appendix B in *Development of Abstractionism* (II-A-7), and traces James's influence on Stein.

153. Horton, Rod W. and Herbert W. Edwards. *Backgrounds of American Literary Thought*. New York: Appleton-Century-Crofts, 1967.

"The great forerunner of the Freudian movement in American literature is Gertrude Stein." *Three Lives* and *The Long Gay Book* anticipated Freud. "Her experiments in automatic writing . . . had led her to the conclusion that beneath the conscious mind lay a deeper, 'other' self (similar to the Freudian unconscious) whose organization was at once more primitive and more nearly common to all men. . . ."

154. Shults, Donald. "Gertrude Stein and the Problems of Time." *Kyushu American Literature* (Fukuoka, Japan), 11 (1968), 59-71.

155. Tufte, Virginia J. "Gertrude Stein's Prothalamium: A Unique Poem in a Classical Mode." *Yale University Library Gazette,* 43 (July 1968), 17-23.

Tufte writes that *Prothalamium for Bobolink and His Louise/Very Well I Thank You/Love Like Anything* "merits a wider audience than the handful of readers who were favored with copies in 1939 and 1940," as it is "the only prothalamium by a major American author."

"It is of special interest because Gertrude Stein, usually the most unconventional of authors, is here drawing heavily on conventional motifs of the classical epithalamium, or 'song at the couch', a literary genre that owes many of its motifs to Sappho. And it is a rarity in twentieth-century American literature in that it is a work which yields its full meaning only when read in the light of conventions that have functioned in European literature for thirty centuries or more."

156. Brown, Ashley. "Going on Being." *Spectator,* 221 (6 December 1968), 800-01.

The occasion of this article is the first British publication of *Making of Americans,* a book which "has had only an 'underground' reputation" because of "the 'expression' of a state of consciousness" which continues for 925 pages.

Brown compares, briefly, Gustave Flaubert's *Un Coeur Simple* and Stein's *Three Lives;* Flaubert uses his own language and style, while Stein uses mostly "the language of her subjects."

157. Schorer, Mark. *The World We Imagine: Selected Essays.* London: Chatto and Windus, 1969.

In "Some Relationships: Gertrude Stein, Sherwood Anderson, F. Scott Fitzgerald, and Ernest Hemingway," Schorer focuses more on the other authors than on Stein, although he is

cognizant of Stein's influence on the other three. "Melanctha"
is "probably Gertrude Stein's most important literary
achievement."

158. Knox, George. "The Great American Novel: Final
Chapter." *American Quarterly,* 21 (Winter 1969),
667-82.

> Knox is concerned with the twentieth-century novel. *The
> Making of Americans* is Stein's "super-spoof of [The Great
> American Novel]." Structurally it is "imitative, utilizing the
> 'chaos' and amorphousness of American life. . . ."
> "The thrust of the effort to *essentialize* American life is anti-
> novelistic, perhaps the first 20th century effort (except for
> Joyce) to universalize." "Although she ironically lamented
> at the age of thirty that she would never write The
> Great American Novel, she nevertheless did. Her attempt was
> a caricature, the effort to create a monumental national 'fiction'
> out of the prescriptive stuff of theory about a particular
> culture. . . . It is perhaps the most elaborate *tour de force* in
> the tradition of The Great American Novel debate, an attempt
> by a 'humorous' artist to resolve the ridiculous universalist-
> localist and nationalist-regionalist conflict—not critically
> but fictionally. . . ."

159. Kesting, Marianne. *Entdeckung und Destruktion: Zur
Strukturumwandlung der Künste.* München: Wilhelm
Fink Verlag, 1970.

> Chapter 12, "Musikalisierung des Theaters—Theatralisierung
> der Musik," appears under the general heading "Vollzug und
> Verhinderung der Bühnenrevolution." Comments on Stein, as
> well as an imprecise translation of a paragraph from "Gradual
> Making of *The Making of Americans,*" appear in Chapter 12.

160. Stewart, Lawrence D. "Hemingway and the
Autobiographies of Alice B. Toklas." *Fitzgerald/
Hemingway Annual 1970.* Ed. Matthew J. Bruccoli and
C.E. Frazer Clark, Jr. Washington, D.C.: NCR
Microcard Editions, 1970. Pp. 117-23.

> Most of the article is based on an interview taped 29 April

1960. Hemingway always omits Toklas's name. This is another of Hemingway's versions vs. that of Toklas/Stein.

161. Katz, Leon. "Matisse, Picasso and Gertrude Stein," in *Four Americans in Paris: The Collections of Gertrude Stein and Her Family*. Ed. Irene Gordon. New York: The Museum of Modern Art, 1970. Pp. 51-63.

See also II-A-5.

162. Katz, Leon and Edward Burns. " 'They Walk in the Light': Gertrude Stein and Pablo Picasso," in *Gertrude Stein on Picasso*. Ed. Edward Burns. New York: Liveright, 1970. Pp. 109-16.

Compare with preceding entry.

163. Gallup, Donald. "Du côté de chez Stein." *Book Collector*, 19 (Summer 1970), 169-84.

"In the Yale Library's Collection of American Literature . . . there is a group of archival materials relating primarily to 20th-century American literary history which owes its presence in New Haven either directly or indirectly to Gertrude Stein." This, then, relates how Stein's letters, manuscripts, and so forth, were left to Yale and how other people (i.e. Carl Van Vechten, Thornton Wilder, to name only two) thus left their memorabilia to Yale. Gallup also relates the story of Stein's talk at Église Réformée in Choisy-le-Roi to a Franco-American audience. This appears to be the only location of this story. Gallup also relates the history of *The Mother of Us All* characters.

164. Bense, Max. "Was erzählt Gertrude Stein?" *Probleme des Erzählens in der Weltliteratur: Festschrift für Käte Hamburger zum 75. Geburtstag am 21. September 1971*. Ed. Fritz Martini. Stuttgart: Ernst Klett Verlag, 1971. Pp. 330-47.

Bense notes nothing new, but his article is perhaps important simply because he notes that Stein moved to "einer strukturellen, musikalischen, rhythmischen, fugenartigen Schreibweise. . . ." His article contains biographical errors;

for example, Gertrude Stein did not translate Gustave Flaubert's *Trois Contes*.

"Sie entdeckte und erprobte vielleicht als erste die ästhetischen Möglichkeiten der Sprache auf deren syntaktischer Ebene. . . ."

"Man versteht die moderne Prosa nicht, wenn man sie nicht in diesem Raum ontologischer, semantischer und syntaktischer Erneuerungen sieht, die durch James Joyce, Franz Kafka und Gertrude Stein wirksam geworden sind, und man versteht auch Gertrude Steins merkwürdige Texte nicht, wenn man sie ausserhalb dieses literarischen Zusammenhangs verstehen will."

Bense is mainly interested in *Making of Americans* and *Tender Buttons*.

165. Cohn, Ruby. *Dialogue in American Drama*. Bloomington: Indiana University Press, 1971.

The discussion of Stein's plays appears in chapter 6, "Less Than Novel," 201-07.

"Her plays have received no attention from drama critics and small attention from Stein critics, but she herself was conscious of writing a radically original kind of drama." Cohn finds social satire in some of the *Geography and Plays* plays, and also examines *Operas and Plays* and *Last Operas and Plays*.

Gertrude Stein's drama is a reaction against the whole dramatic tradition. In order to plunge the reader-spectator into the immediate *thereness* of her continuous present, Stein stripped her plays of plot, character, event, theme, subject, and meaningful dialogue. Instead, she gives us disjunctive and rhythmic dialogue, often spoken by undesignated voices. Disoriented, we must respond to the words' immediacy. Sometimes the linguistic exploration in the dialogue takes a spatial form in the theater. Though Stein was probably not familiar with the work of [Adolphe] Appia, Artland, [Edward Gordon] Craig, or [Vserolod Emilievich] Meyerhold, she too was engaged in spatializing the theater. But her space was filled with words, estranged from their denotative meaning.

166. Hoffman, Frederick J. "Gertrude Stein," in
Encyclopedia of World Literature in the Twentieth Century.
Ed. Wolfgang Bernard Fleischmann. New York:
Ungar, 1971.

This is a short and imprecise biographical and bibliographical sketch which sees Stein's principal role as "tutor and example, not writer."

167. Mayhall, Jane. "Gertrude Stein's *Things As They Are*,"
in *Rediscoveries: Informal Essays in Which Well-Known
Novelists Rediscover Neglected Works of Fiction by One of
Their Favorite Authors.* Ed. David Madden. New York:
Crown, 1971. Pp. 198-208.

"Here may be, after all, Stein's most daring book."
"*Things As They Are* is a new and shocking book, written in 1903. It is shocking because it does not presume to be shocking. It is new, because the departure from the old seems neither premediated nor manufactured. . . . What she had produced in this, her first novel, was neither experiment nor exercise, but a highly developed species, already bursting with life and demands." Stein "is saved by a streak of sensuality" from "the lures of philosophy" in *Things As They Are*; "her natural sense of comedy" also saves the book.
"Her style seems pivotal. Not only is there a lack of nineteenth-century embellishment, but the dialogue is amazingly contemporary, audacious. . . ."

168. Starke, Catherine Juanita. *Black Portraiture in
American Fiction: Stock Characters, Archetypes, and
Individuals.* New York: Basic Books, 1971.

Oliver Eugene, the main character of Henry Van Dyke's *Blood of Strawberries* (New York: Farrar, Straus and Giroux, 1968), admires Stein and listens to *Four Saints in Three Acts*. Between pp. 183-86, Melanctha is discussed as a "transitional figure," "a complex portrait of a Negro in transition from cultural determinism to individualistic self-assertion."

169. Sutherland, Donald. "Gertrude Stein and the Twentieth Century," in *A Primer for the Gradual Understanding of Gertrude Stein*. Ed. Robert Bartlett Haas. Los Angeles: Black Sparrow Press, 1971. Pp. 139-56.

170. Cooper, Douglas. "Gertrude Stein and Juan Gris." *Apollo*, 93 (January 1971), 28-35.

Cooper's article also appears in *Four Americans in Paris: The Collections of Gertrude Stein and Her Family*, ed. Irene Gordon (II-A-5). He recounts the relationship between Stein and Gris. See Daniel-Henry Kahnweiler, I-B-ii-58, I-B-iii-42, II-D-14.

171. Alloway, Lawrence. "Art." *Nation*, 212 (11 January 1971), 61-62.

This article concerns *Four Americans in Paris, Picasso*, and the contents of the collection. Alloway devotes several paragraphs responding to Douglas Cooper's article (see preceding entry) and to what he finds tiresome (incorrect dates).

172. Rosenberg, Harold. "Paris Annexed." *New Yorker*, 46 (30 January 1971), 71-75.

See *Re-Definition of Art*, by Rosenberg (II-G-9).

173. Ashbery, John. "G.M.P." *Art News*, 69 (February 1971), 44-47 +.

Ashbery gives the background of the Stein Art Collection Show at the Museum of Modern Art. He deals mainly with the Stein-Picasso relationship.

In her book on Picasso, Gertrude Stein tells us that the early years of Cubism were years of gaiety, and that the gaiety ended when Picasso left Montmartre in 1912. The move itself can't have been the cause—in fact Picasso moved to Montparnasse, nearer to where Gertrude lived, which must have pleased her. Perhaps it has something to do with the fact that Cubism was now in full flower, and there was nothing much to look forward to except endless chains of masterpieces. Gertrude Stein said that Picasso achieved "perfection" and "total mastery" in the paintings of 1914–17, and in fact the last period of Cubism has never looked so gorgeous and provocative as in this show. But ripeness and amplitude imply decline, even if it is a great distance off. . . .

174. Cox, James M. "Autobiography and America." *Virginia Quarterly Review*, 47 (Spring 1971), 252-77.

Pages 276-77 are on Stein; the rest of the article is on Benjamin Franklin, Henry David Thoreau, Walt Whitman and Henry Adams. Stein "is the woman whom Adams had tried to imagine emerging from the American scene."

"Gertrude Stein sought an absolute present in which not the life would be everything, the words nothing—as in Whitman—but the words everything and the life nothing. The abstraction of language would be the total present, and the achievement of the writer would lie in disconnecting language from referential reality, thereby making the words upon the page not true but real, not possessed of but possessing total reality in and of themselves. . . ." Stein "united both autobiographical and biographical consciousness in a single creative act. . . ."

175. Stevenson, Florence. "A Continuous Present." *Opera News*, 35 (10 April 1971), 8-13.

Stevenson writes around Stein's "continuous present," presenting mostly biographical and critical notes more easily attainable elsewhere.

176. Fleming, Shirley. "Gertrude Stein, Master Librettist: When This You See. . . ." *High Fidelity and Musical America*, 21 (November 1971), MA 10-11.

Fleming reviews the After Dinner Opera Company's presentation of five short works by Stein, "When This You See Remember Me," composed by six different people. "The impact of the Stein words, during much of the evening, surpassed that of the piano scores (one with additional oboe) that accompanied. . . . The scores, all quite singable in a contemporary, anonymous, craggy way . . . seldom interfering with the basic shape impeding action, and not adding very

much either. . . ." The works were *In a Garden*, music by
Meyer Kupferman; *Three Sisters Who Are Not Sisters*, Ned
Rorem; *Look and Long*, Florence Wickham and Marvin
Schwartz; *Ladies Voices*, Vernon Martin; and *Photograph—1920*,
Martin Kalmanoff. Fleming considers the last two works
the best.

177. Smith, Patrick J. "Gertrude Stein, Master
  Librettist: The Mother of Us All." *High Fidelity and
  Musical America*, 21 (November 1971), MA 10.

This is a review of Hunter College's presentation of *Mother of
Us All*.

178. Kawin, Bruce F. *Telling It Again and Again: Repetition
  in Literature and Film*. Ithaca, New York: Cornell
  University Press, 1972.

Kawin discusses language and repetition, "an aesthetic
device in literature and film, and as a state of mind." Section 4
is particularly concerned with Stein. Kawin compares *Three
Lives* ("Melanctha") with Samuel Beckett's *Watt*, and mentions
"Miss Furr and Miss Skeene," *As A Wife Has a Cow; Four Saints in
Three Acts* is used as an example of her plays which "move in
phase." She "presents motions that stay in place."

179. Stewart, Lawrence D. "Gertrude Stein and the Vital
  Dead." *Mystery and Detection Annual*, 1 (1972), 102-23.

180. Copley, Frank O. "Aristotle to Gertrude Stein: The
  Arts of Poetry." *Mosaic*, 5 (Summer 1972), 85-102.

Stein is discussed between pp. 92-94 and 100-01. Copley uses
Stein's theory of "calling upon names" to explicate some
lyrics. Copley discusses various definitions of poetry and of
prose, and writes: "For the first time [in Stein's theories], the
definitions [of poetry and of prose] do not overlap."

181. Shapiro, Harriet. *"Four Saints in Three Acts." Intellectual
  Digest*, October 1972, pp. 22-26.

Shapiro interviews Virgil Thomson about the creation of *Four
Saints in Three Acts*. "The original attraction ["in Gertrude Stein's

words"] was the strangeness; second was how fantastically
funny it could be; and third was how many interesting layers of
meaning there could be underneath the strangeness and the
funniness."

182. Fendelman, Earl. "Gertrude Stein among the
   Cubists." *Journal of Modern Literature*, 2 (November
   1972), 481-90.
   Basically concerned with *The Autobiography of Alice B. Toklas*,
   Fendelman's article is a partial rewrite of a chapter in his
   dissertation.

183. Brooks, Cleanth, R.W.B. Lewis and Robert Penn
   Warren. "Gertrude Stein," in *American Literature: The
   Makers and the Making*. New York: St. Martin's Press,
   1973. Pp. 2221-37.
   The "Biographical Chart" and "Further Readings" are
   substandard. Nothing more recent than John Malcolm
   Brinnin's *Third Rose* (I-B-i-2) is listed, and the biographical
   data in the chart is so scant as to give many false impressions.
   Selections from *Three Lives, Making of Americans* and *Tender
   Buttons* are included.

184. Cowley, Malcolm. *A Second Flowering: Works and Days
   of the Lost Generation*. New York: Viking, 1973.
   Stein is only mentioned, and mostly in conjunction with
   Ernest Hemingway.

185. Garvin, Harry Raphael. "The Human Mind and
   Tender Buttons." *Widening Circle*, 1, No. 4 (1973),
   11-13.

186. Stewart, Allegra. "Flat Land As Explanation."
   Widening Circle, 1, No. 4 (1973), 31-33 and 22.

187. Maynard, Reid. "Abstractionism in Gertrude Stein's
   Three Lives." *Ball State University Forum*, 15, No. 1 (1973),
   68-71.

188. Nazzaro, Linda. " 'A Piece of Coffee': A Stylistic
     Description of the Work of Gertrude Stein." *English
     Review*, 1 (1973), 50-54.

189. George, Jonathan C. "Stein's 'A Box'." *Explicator*, 31
     (February 1973), No. 42.

> "A Box" is one of the "Objects" in Tender Buttons. In an
> interesting explication, George writes: "Throughout the
> poem diction is kept extremely simple, yet words are used with
> a lexical precision which is often at odds with customary
> usage. . . . The frequent progressive verb forms, passive
> voice, and infinitive mode imply a world of condition rather
> than action, and, above all, a world without causation.
> Indeed, this latter characteristic is the most revolutionary
> and disturbing feature of Miss Stein's style in this poem—
> the denial of that sense of agency or causation on which all
> traditional syntax is based."

190. Fitz, L. T. "Gertrude Stein and Picasso: The
     Language of Surfaces." *American Literature*, 45
     (May 1973), 228-37.

> ". . . Stein's selection of [Pablo Picasso's] important
> periods is interesting to us because it sheds light on her own
> work. It is my feeling that this cubist-flatness struggle
> which Stein saw as being so important to Picasso is present
> in her own work and is one key to her sometimes puzzling
> style.
> "These are, I believe, three things which Stein's style
> shares with Picasso's: 1) a cubist approach; 2) a style which
> concentrates on what is seen rather than what is remembered;
> and 3) a calligraphic or nonsymbolic concept of language."
> Stein had three styles: "objective"; "paraphrasable"; and
> "a style that makes no syntactical sense," i.e.
> "unparaphrasable." In her third style, Stein treats "words
> as things in themselves. She enjoyed not the meaning of a
> word but the way it sounded; not the meaning of a
> line but the look of a printed line on a page."
> "In the end it was her creation of the thing contained
> within itself for which we remember her. Her brilliant
> surfaces will shine long after her calligraphy has been
> forgotten."

191. Gass, William H. "Gertrude Stein, Geographer: I."
New York Review of Books, 3 May 1973, 5-8.

> This and the following make up Gass's introduction to
> *Geographical History of America*.

192. ———. "Gertrude Stein, Geographer: II." *New
York Review of Books*, 17 May 1973, 25-29.

193. McCaffrey, John. " 'Any of Mine Without Music to
Help Them': The Operas and Plays of Gertrude
Stein." *Yale/Theatre*, 4 No. 3 (Summer 1973), 27-39.

> McCaffrey reviews *In Circles, Four Saints in Three Acts,*
> *Mother of Us All*, and the After Dinner Opera Co. presentations.
> He presents a history of Gertrude Stein in music, emphasizing
> contemporary reviews of contemporary efforts. Al Carmines's
> operas are mentioned, as is Nancy Cole and *Dr. Faustus*.

194. *White Pelican: A Quarterly Review of the Arts* (Edmonton,
Alberta), 3 (Autumn 1973).

> Most of this issue is devoted to Gertrude Stein, who
> influenced The Four Horsemen, "the Toronto-based group who
> perform the most advanced and exciting sound poetry."
> The "Editorial," pp. 4-5, is partially on the Gertrude Stein
> section of the Edinburgh festival. *White Pelican* also
> includes "Stein-influenced poetry and graphics from" Steve
> McCaffrey and bp Nichol. Pp. 6-14 contain "Gertrude Stein: The
> Style Is the Machine" by Sheila Watson. Also included:
> F. Scott Taylor, "By Design: Gertrude Stein," pp. 34-37;
> Shirley Swartz, "Between Autobiographies: Gertrude Stein and
> the Problem of Audience," pp. 40-47; Steve McCaffrey,
> "Prefatory Notes on Stein and the Language Hygene
> Programme," pp. 50-60; and an article by bp Nichol which
> "is excerpted from some beginning writings on GERTRUDE
> STEIN'S THEORIES OF PERSONALITY . . . ," pp. 15-23.
> This issue of *White Pelican* is very interesting and thought-
> provoking.

195. Klaitch, Dolores. *Woman + Woman: Attitudes toward
Lesbianism*. New York: Morrow, 1974.

> Some of Stein's works are, of course, much more

comprehensible when the reader realizes Gertrude's
relationship with Alice B. Toklas was of a lesbian nature.
Klaitch writes about *Q.E.D.*, *Bee Time Vine* (in particular,
"Lifting Belly" and "A Sonatina Followed by Another"),
"Miss Furr and Miss Skeene," and *A Long Gay Book*. The latter
discussion is based on the speculation that "the word 'gay' came
to be used to denote things homosexual" "as early as 1908."

Klaitch also includes a portion of a letter from a female
editor of Stein (Patricia Meyerowitz), in which the woman
denies any possibility of a lesbian attachment between
Gertrude and Alice. (See I-B-iii-81).

Klaitch's book is important, timely, rational, and well
researched. Without meaning this as a comment on the whole,
one wonders, however, if the realization that "Toklas was one
strong dyke" adds anything to one's understanding of Stein,
Toklas, Stein's work, or lesbianism.

196. Kanazeki, Hisao. "Gertrude Stein and the Atomic
     Bomb." *The Rising Generation*, 120 (1974), 418-19.

197. Shaw, Sharon. "Gertrude Stein and Henry James:
     The Difference between Accidence and Coincidence."
     Pembroke Magazine, 5 (1974), 95-101.

198. Schmitz, Neil. "Gertrude Stein as Post-Modernist:
     The Rhetoric of *Tender Buttons*." *Journal of Modern
     Literature*, 3 (July 1974), 1203-18.

"My purpose in this essay is to establish the meaning of
Gertrude Stein's mode in her text, the core of its linguistic
pact, and to set that mode within the context of
contemporary narrative." Michael Hoffman's approach results
in "a reading of the text that ultimately dismisses itself."
Approaching *Tender Buttons* "as a psychological experiment
begins by necessarily amputating the element of its style."

"After *Tender Buttons* she ceased to ask the technical questions
about story and character so current in modern writing. . . .
she did not . . . abandon the socio-political realm."

Schmitz's is a contrived reading of *Tender Buttons*; his
analogies are somewhat suspect.

199. Cooper, David D. "Gertrude Stein's 'Magnificent Asparagus': Horizontal Vision and Unmeaning in 'Tender Buttons'." *Modern Fiction Studies*, 20 (Autumn 1974), 337-49.

> In a Jungian approach to Stein, Cooper writes that *Tender Buttons*, like *Ulysses*, "turns its back on us; it is uncooperative; it defies contradiction."
> *Tender Buttons* has similarities with Carl Jung's " 'visionary' model." Stein was not interested "either to *ascend* or *descend* into the essence of 'Self'. She is more interested . . . in focusing all her creative energy on a moment in time and assessing that moment linearly—all in order to 'pull in' fragmented bits of sensation that so often slip by the normalized process of perception. . . . "
> ". . . I think that her point is *un-meaning*."

200. *Lost Generation Journal*, 2 (Winter 1974).

> This entire issue is devoted to Stein.

201. Bradbury, Malcolm and David Corker. "The American Risorgimento: The Coming of the New Arts," in *History of Literature in the English Language. Vol. 9: American Literature Since 1900*. Ed. Marcus Cunliffe. London: Sphere Books, 1975. Pp. 17-47.

> This book was in manuscript form in 1971, which might explain why the bibliographical section on Stein is so inadequate.

202. Frieling, Kenneth. "The Becoming of Gertrude Stein's *The Making of Americans*," in *The Twenties: Fiction, Poetry, Drama*. Ed. Warren French. Deland, Florida: Everett/Edwards, 1975. Pp. 157-70.

> The bibliography is very brief. The article, however brief, is an interesting and new discussion of *Making of Americans*.

203. Kenner, Hugh. *A Homemade World: The American Modernist Writers.* New York: Knopf, 1975.

"Pressed flat into ritual symmetries, that was how Miss Stein intuited twentieth-century language. . . . She was the [Piet] Mondrian of prose, and her intuitions were often profound, even as her prose was often unreadable. Her prose was resisting a drag toward lyric nostalgia."

204. McMillan, Dougald. *transition: The History of a Literary Era 1927-1938.* London: Calder and Boyars, 1975.

The main section on Gertrude Stein occurs in part 3, "The Figures of the Cause"—pp. 167-78. There are also innumerable comments and details strewn throughout the whole book, as well as a great deal of information on *transition*, pre-World War II Paris and the other important writers who were there. Of especial interest is the first appendix, "Title pages of *transition* 1-27," pp. 235-78.

205. Spencer, Benjamin T. "Gertrude Stein: Non-Expatriate," in *Literature and Ideas in America: Essays in Memory of Harry Hayden Clark*, ed. Robert Falk. Oberlin: Ohio University Press, 1975. Pp. 204-27.

Concerns Stein's preoccupation with the United States of America.

206. Wasserstrom, William. "The Sursymamericubealism of Gertrude Stein." *Twentieth Century Literature,* 21 (February 1975), 90-106.

This article is at times acute, glib, witty—sometimes too ("a rose" . . . . "arose")—and inaccurate: "Imagine Gertrude Stein in 1925 writing *Making of Americans.* . . ." Wasserstrom disagrees with James M. Cox and "Stein as a direct descendant of [Henry] Adams":" . . . her whole *oeuvre* has the effect of setting right all Adams's miscalculations of history, his whole cosmology." She denies many of Adams's views, negates him, contradicts him.

"Wherever one turned, in opera, ballet, theatre, painting, literary theory and practice—there she was. . . . If circumambience is a reliable gauge of power then Hugh Kenner is wrong: all those extravaganzas of art in which Gertrude Stein shared from 1900 to the Second World War identify a Stein era not a [André] Breton or a [Ezra] Pound era."

207. Alkon, Paul. "Visual Rhetoric in *The Autobiography of Alice B. Toklas.*" *Critical Inquiry*, 1 (June 1975), 849-81.

This is a very good and interesting article on the placement of photographs in the American first edition of *Autobiography of Alice B. Toklas* and how they function. "Past, present and future are reversed. . . ."

208. Wood, Carl. "Continuity of Romantic Irony: Stein's Homage to Laforgue in *Three Lives.*" *Comparative Literature Studies*, 12, No. 2 (June 1975), 147-58.

209. Steiner, Wendy. "The Steinian Portrait." *Yale University Library Gazette*, 50 (July 1975), 30-40.

Ms. Steiner presents in this article some of her "findings" in her dissertation (II-B-21). Following her article, "Three Hitherto Unpublished Portraits" are printed (pp. 41-45).

210. Moers, Ellen. *Literary Women.* New York: Doubleday, 1976.

Moers talks about Stein in the context of women writers, women's literature, and so on; this is a very insubstantial mention.

211. Rule, Jane. "Gertrude Stein." *Lesbian Images.* New York: Pocket Books, 1976. Pp. 64-76.

Lesbian Images was first published in 1975.
"*Q.E.D.* is probably the only book about lesbian relationship which confronts its characters with the raw war between desire and morality and reveals the psychological geometry of the human heart without false romanticizing or easy judgment." Touching on *Three Lives*, Richard Bridgman's suggestions as to Stein's movement towards abstractionism, and *Tender Buttons*, Rule writes: "*Tender Buttons* is probably

not code at all, though certainly some words have private
and charged sexual meaning for Gertrude Stein. It is more
likely that this is a serious if not altogether satisfying
experiment to dislodge words from any meaning, personal
or public, to create arbitrary aesthetic pleasure from their
being grouped together." Rule mentions *Autobiography of
Alice B. Toklas* and considers the implications *if* it were a
collaboration.

212. Rother, James. "Gertrude Stein and the Translation
of Experience." *Essays in Literature* (Iowa University), 3
(1976), 105-18.

213. Schmitt-von Mühlenfels, Franz. "Zur Einwirkung
des Kubismus auf de französische und nordameri-
kanische Literatur." *Arcadia: Zeitschrift für vergleichende
Literaturwissenschaft*, 11 (1976), 238-55.

Gertrude Stein and her works, especially *Tender Buttons*, are
discussed on pp. 247-50. Schmitt-von Mühlenfels points out that
so-called cubistic elements already exist in Stein's work before
cubism developed. "Jedoch könnte man in der funktionalen
Behandlung repetitorischer Sprachelemente innerhalb eines
Textzusammenhangs, in dem eine multiperspektivische
Umsetzung von Informationsfragmenten im Rahmen eines
autonomen, der Alltagssprache entrückten Literaturwerkes
stattfindet, durchaus eine Einwirkung kubistischer Technik
sehen." And, in the next sentence, "Eine direkte Einwirkung
des Kubismus nicht nur in stilistischer, sondern auch in
thematischer Hinsicht liegt schliesslich in . . . *Tender
Buttons* vor." In discussing "A Table," Schmitt makes the
following point: "die Analogie zur kubistischen Technik
läge dann darin, dass die semantischen Grundvorstellungen des
Stabilen und des Unstabilen in verschiedenen perspektivischen
Brechungen erscheinen. . . . Das Objekt 'Tisch' wird bei
Gertrude Stein imaginativ in ein rein innersprachliches
Phänomen verwandelt, es wird zum Textobjekt nach quasi
kubistischen Bauprinzipien und stellt damit ein Beispiel eines
literarischen Kubismus dar, wie er in dieser Ausgeprägtheit
wohl nur bei Gertrude Stein vorkommt. . . ." Schmitt-von
Mühlenfels's article is not a major one, but is definitely
interesting.

214. Brady, Ruth H. "Stein's 'A Long Dress'."
     Explicator, 34, No. 6 (February 1976), No. 47.

215. Kornfeld, Lawrence. "From a Director's Notebook:
     How the Curtain Did Come: Conflict and Change.
     The Theatre of Gertrude Stein." *Performing Arts
     Journal*, 1, No. 1 (Spring 1976), 33-39.
     Kornfeld directed six of Stein's plays between 1957 and 1974;
     here he presents his approach to them.

216. Farber, Lawren. "Fading: A Way. Gertrude Stein's
     Sources for *Three Lives*." *Journal of Modern Literature*, 5
     (September 1976), 463-80.
     Farber construes and examines an etymological and a
     theological background for each of *The Three Lives*, and draws
     the subsequent moral from each story. This article leads
     to a contrived reading of Stein. His suppositions become Stein's
     conscious choices as the article advances.

217. Thau, Annette. "Max Jacob's Letters to Gertrude
     Stein: A Critical Study." Max Jacob Centennial
     Issue. *Folio: Papers on Foreign Languages and Literatures*,
     9 (October 1976), 47-54.
     Seven letters written between 1923 and 1939 and Thau's
     analysis of the Jacob-Stein relationship are presented here.

218. Couser, G. Thomas. "Of Time and Identity: Walt
     Whitman and Gertrude Stein as Autobiographers."
     Texas Studies in Language and Literature, 17, No. 4
     (Winter 1976), 787-804.

219. Rose, Marilyn Gaddis. "Gertrude Stein and Cubist
     Narrative." *Modern Fiction Studies*, 22 (Winter
     1976/77), 543-55.
     Despite some unfortunate errors ("Bridges" for Bridgman,
     for example), this is an interesting study of *Three Lives*,
     Lucy Church Amiably, and *Ida*.

220. Lodge, David. "Gertrude Stein," in *The Modes of Modern Writing: Metaphor, Metonymy, and the Typology of Modern Literature*. London: Edward Arnold, 1977. Pp. 144-55.

Lodge concentrates on *Three Lives, Making of Americans*, and *Long Gay Book* in his discussion of Stein as modernist writer. Chapters on Ernest Hemingway and Virginia Woolf, among others, also contain references to Stein.

221. Steiner, Wendy. "Gertrude Stein in Manuscript." *Yale University Library Gazette*, 51 (January 1977), 156-63.

Steiner points out the correlation between Stein's notebook covers and their contents in "at least thirteen cases" between 1923 and 1930. She uses "He and They, Hemingway" as a case in point and explicates the piece. This very good article is followed by "The Leo D. Stein Papers" (pp. 164-66).

222. Stimpson, Catharine R. "The Mind, the Body, and Gertrude Stein." *Critical Inquiry*, 3 (Spring 1977), 489-506.

An interesting study of sexuality in the works of Stein, especially in *Fernhurst,Q.E.D., Three Lives* and *Making of Americans*.

223. Fleissner, Robert F. "Stein's Four Roses." *Journal of Modern Literature*, 6 (April 1977), 325-28.

This is a flippant attempt "to find the meaning . . . of Stein's poetic four roses," which Stein did much better. Fleissner quotes Greenfeld's quotations of Stein.

"I submit that there are as many meanings as there are roses. . . . There are, briefly, (1) the impressionistic, (2) the technical, (3) the meaning of the rose itself, and (4) the analogical."

ADDENDUM

224. Malone, Kemp. "Observations on *Paris France.*"
Papers on Language and Literature, 3 (Spring 1967),
159-78.

Basically an analysis and explication of *Paris France,* this
article examines the various and sundry topics in the book
and ends with some observations on Stein's style. Malone
includes some interesting word counts. He speaks of Stein in
connection with the theatre of the absurd. Malone's language is
sometimes nebulous, but this may be caused by the specific
paragraph or topic under discussion.

D. Introductions to Stein's Works

1. Anderson, Sherwood. "The Work of Gertrude Stein." *Little Review*, 8 (Spring 1922), 29-32.

    In his introduction to *Geography and Plays*, Anderson, defending Stein, approaches her work "as the most important pioneer work done in the field of letters in my time."

2. Van Vechten, Carl. "Introduction." *Three Lives*, by Gertrude Stein. New York: Modern Library, 1933. Pp. v-xi.

    This is a history of *Three Lives*, which had a "striking underground reputation," and a history of Van Vechten's appreciation and reading of Stein. *Three Lives* is "a masterpiece" and the "author's first book." "Melanctha" is "an authentic milestone on the long road of American letters."

3. Faÿ, Bernard. "Preface." *The Making of Americans*, by Gertrude Stein. New York: Harcourt, Brace and World, 1934. Pp. ix-xxiii.

    Faÿ's introduction to the abridged edition contains many misconceptions. See II-E-xii-1.

4. Wilder, Thornton. "Introduction." *Narration*, by Gertrude Stein. Chicago: University of Chicago Press, 1935. Pp. v-vii.

    Wilder's introductions to Stein's works are accepted as among the best to appear.

5. ———. "Introduction." *The Geographical History of America Or the Relation of Human Nature to the Human Mind*. New York: Random House, 1936.

    This introduction is reprinted in the Vintage edition of *Geographical History*, published in 1973, pp. 43-50. See II-D-25.

6. Haas, Robert Bartlett. "Another Garland for Gertrude Stein." *What Are Masterpieces*, by Gertrude Stein. Los

Angeles: Conference Press, 1940. Pp. 9-22.

Haas quotes the dust-jacket of *Geography and Plays* in order
to provide biographical information. His introduction to
Stein and her career is fairly well done.

7. Van Vechten, Carl. "A Stein Song." *Selected Writings
of Gertrude Stein.* Ed. Carl Van Vechten. New York:
Random House, 1946. Pp. xviii-xxiv.

Van Vechten attempts to present a history of Stein's writing
career, i.e, a history of her different styles.

8. Wilder, Thornton. "Introduction." *Four in America,*
by Gertrude Stein. New Haven: Yale University
Press, 1947. Pp. v-xxvii.

Wilder's introduction contains some inaccuracies. Despite
these, it is a sound introduction to Stein's work in general.

9. Van Vechten, Carl. "How Many Acts Are There in
It?" *Last Operas and Plays,* by Gertrude Stein. New
York: Rinehart, 1949. Pp. vii-xix.

Van Vechten gives a history of the plays contained in this
volume.

10. Flanner, Janet. "Frame for Some Portraits." *Two:
Gertrude Stein and Her Brother and Other Early Portraits
(1908-1912).* New Haven: Yale University Press, 1951.
Pp. ix-xvii.

"Frame"= "ideas which Miss Stein talked on and which
were her ideas about her readers and about her portraits
for her readers to read." See II-E-xxxii-5.

11. Frankenberg, Lloyd. "On First Meeting Mrs.
Reynolds." *Mrs. Reynolds and Five Earlier Novelettes
(1931-1942),* by Gertrude Stein. New Haven: Yale
University Press, 1952. Pp. v-xii.

Frankenberg "suggest[s] some of the paradoxes and
apparent contradictions in her life and art." Mostly he asks

a number of questions which "are addressed to the scholar who will one day try to pin them all down."

12. Thomson, Virgil. "Preface." *Bee Time Vine and Other Pieces (1913-1927)*, by Gertrude Stein. New Haven: Yale University Press, 1953.

Thomson wrote the preface and notes for this, the third volume of *The Yale Edition of the Unpublished Writings of Gertrude Stein*. The notes are due, in part, to Toklas's information and remembrances. Thomson says that "the greatness of the great poets has never been measurable by the amount of clear thought expressed in their works. It is far more a matter of their ability to compose unforgettable lines. Judged by this standard Gertrude Stein ranks very high indeed."

This volume is by far the most difficult of this series to read. Thomson intersperses commentary among the poems; one reads Thomson followed by Stein followed by Thomson ad infinitum. Compare this inadequate technique with that of Robert Bartlett Haas (II-D-6) or Patricia Meyerowitz (II-D-23).

13. Barney, Natalie Clifford. "Foreword." *As Fine As Melanctha (1914-1930)*, by Gertrude Stein. New Haven: Yale University Press, 1954. Pp. vii-xix.

This rather long "foreword" does not forward one's understanding of Gertrude Stein. Barney refers to "my personal experience and points of contact and discord with this author, whose companionship I delighted in and now cherish."

"Her repetitions" . . . "seem to me just a way of marking time before finding out what to say next," which, Barney continues, is not necessarily negative.

14. Kahnweiler, Daniel-Henry. "Introduction." Trans. Donald Gallup. *Painted Lace and Other Pieces (1914-1937)*, by Gertrude Stein. New Haven: Yale University Press, 1955. Pp. ix-xviii.

Kahnweiler reports on the history of his relationship with Gertrude Stein and Alice B. Toklas and of his publishing books with Stein.

15. Sutherland, Donald. "Preface: The Turning Point." *Stanzas in Meditation and Other Poems (1929-1933)*, by Gertrude Stein. New Haven: Yale University Press, 1956. Pp. v-xxiv.

   Sutherland presents a history of Stein's style, particularly 1929-1933, the "climax of her heroic experimentation with the essentials of writing." He is most concerned with "Stanzas in Meditation," although the other selections are also discussed. Meaning and language are discussed, and Sutherland attempts to translate some of Stein's lines, but in doing so seems only to make these lines more complicated.

16. Gallup, Donald. "Introduction." *Alphabets and Birthdays*, by Gertrude Stein. New Haven: Yale University Press, 1957. Pp. vii-xix.

   Gallup's "Introduction" is a bibliographical history of *Alphabets and Birthdays;* he relates when and how the pieces were written, and why *To Do: A Book of Alphabets and Birthdays* was not published as a book. Stein's writings for children are discussed.

   Gallup thinks that, since this volume is a cross-section of writings, it might serve "as an introduction to other volumes already published in this series." As an assuredly very important member of the advisory committee for the Yale Edition (Donald Sutherland and Thornton Wilder being the other two; Carl Van Vechten was general editor), one wonders why Gallup did not have this volume published first. This introduction also contains one of Gallup's rare errors. He writes that "the final piece in this volume is the latest in time of composition." "History Or Messages from History" (p. 219) was, however, written in 1930, according to the "Key to the *Yale Catalogue*" (in I-A-i-4). The first piece, *To Do,* was written in 1940, as Gallup himself states in the "Introduction" and according to the *Yale Catalogue.* (The other five pieces appearing in *Alphabets and Birthdays* were written between 1916 and 1927 and, of those five, three were composed in 1924.)

17. Van Vechten, Carl. "A Few Words à propos of a 'Little' *Novel of Thank You.*" *A Novel of Thank You,* by Gertrude Stein. New Haven: Yale University Press, 1958. Pp. vii-xiv.

    One of the best articles Van Vechten has written on Stein, this is basically concerned with bibliographical information. Alice B.Toklas helped with the notes in the introduction.

18. Dupee, F. W. "Gertrude Stein." *Commentary,* 33 (June 1962), 519-23.

    The "general introduction" to *Selected Writings of Gertrude Stein,* ed. Carl Van Vechten (New York: Random House, 1962), is also reprinted in F. W. Dupee, "It Shows Shine: Notes on Gertrude Stein," in *"The King of Cats" and Other Remarks on Writers and Writing.* New York: Farrar, Straus, Giroux, 1965, pp. 69-79.

    "Gnomic, repetitive, illogical, sparsely punctuated, this idiom ['Steinese'] became a scandal and a delight, lending itself to derisory parody and fierce denunciation."

19. Harrison, Gilbert A. "Introduction." *Gertrude Stein's America.* Ed. Gilbert A. Harrison. New York: Liveright, 1965.

20. Brinnin, John Malcolm. "Introduction." *Selected Operas and Plays of Gertrude Stein.* Ed. John Malcolm Brinnin. Pittsburgh: University of Pittsburgh Press, 1970. Pp. xi-xvii.

    Stein's plays are "an almost improbable mixture of primitive mindlessness and sophisticated intellect. Their primitivism shows a ritual gesture, the sing-song incantations of children, sequences of talk, and exchanges of dialogue so little ordered that they might have been picked at random by a tape recorder placed in the center of a crowd. Their sophistication lies in the fact that, without being ideological, they are always conceptual, always based in a governing idea even though that idea may be all but dissolved in the presentation."

    Brinnin discusses landscape, and pays some attention to *Dr. Faustus, Yes Is for a Very Young Man,* and *Mother of Us All.*

21. Katz, Leon. "Introduction." *Fernhurst,Q.E.D., and Other Early Writings,* by Gertrude Stein. New York: Liveright, 1971. Pp. ix-xlii.

    "With the exception of *Q.E.D.,* the writings collected in this volume are apprentice work, but through them lies the way to an understanding of one of this century's most original creative innovators. The inherent logic of Stein's work, probably more than that of any writer of our time, has to be understood by recovering its chronology."

    Katz's is an excellent introduction to Stein's work. See especially II-B-13, from which the material for this introduction was taken.

22. Haas, Robert Bartlett. "Preface." *A Primer for the Gradual Understanding of Gertrude Stein.* Ed. Robert Bartlett Haas. Los Angeles: Black Sparrow Press, 1971.

23. Meyerowitz, Patricia. "Editor's Foreword." *Look at Me Now and Here I Am: Writings and Lectures 1909-45,* by Gertrude Stein. Ed. Patricia Meyerowitz. Harmondsworth: Penguin Books, 1971.

    This book first appeared as *Gertrude Stein: Writings and Lectures 1909-1945* (London: Peter Owen, 1967). Meyerowitz's "Preface" leads this compiler to believe there are differences between the two editions.

24. Sprigge, Elizabeth. "Introduction." *Look at Me Now and Here I Am: Writings and Lectures 1909-45,* by Gertrude Stein. Ed. Patricia Meyerowitz. Harmondsworth: Penguin Books, 1971. Pp. 11-17.

    Sprigge writes a very brief, and very inadequate, biographical sketch as an introduction to Stein's writings.

25. Gass, William H. "Introduction to the Vintage Edition." *The Geographical History of America Or The Relation of Human Nature to the Human Mind,* by Gertrude Stein. New York: Vintage, 1973. Pp. 3-42.

    Gass's introduction is very good. There are, however, several errors. He incorrectly assigns the following quotation to Daniel Stein: "Little Gertie is a little schnatterer. . . ." (John Malcolm Brinnin has it in the following form: "Our little Gertie is a little Schnatterer. . . .") Elizabeth Sprigge attributes the quotation to Rachel Keyser, and Brinnin says it was in a letter sent to Daniel Stein.

26. Haas, Robert Bartlett. "Gertrude Stein's 'Space of Time Filled with Moving'." *Volume I of the Previously Uncollected Writings of Gertrude Stein: Reflection on the Atomic Bomb.* Ed. Robert Bartlett Haas. Los Angeles: Black Sparrow Press, 1973.

   The annotations to this and the following item are much better than either introduction.

27. ———. "Gertrude Stein's 'Sense of the Immediate'." *Volume II of the Previously Uncollected Writings of Gertrude Stein: How Writing Is Written.* Ed. Robert Bartlett Haas. Los Angeles: Black Sparrow Press, 1974.

28. Meyerowitz, Patricia. "Preface" and "Introduction to the Dover Edition." *How to Write,* by Gertrude Stein. New York: Dover, 1975.

   "I decided to use the words of Gertrude Stein together with my own comments to see whether I could convey some of the ideas which occupied the thoughts of Gertrude Stein and also how she approached writing as a creative activity."

Translations of Stein's works are frequently supplied with forewords, afterwords or introductions. See I-A-i-7 for Stein in translation. Cesare Pavese's prefaces to *The Autobiography of Alice B. Toklas* and to *Three Lives* were translated by him and appear in *American Literature: Essays and Opinions* (Berkeley: University of California Press, 1970), pp. 153-64.

E. Reviews of Stein's Works

i. Three Lives (1909)

1. Anon. "Fiction, but Not Novels." *Kansas City Star*, 18 December 1909, p. 5.

James Mellow, in *Charmed Circle* (I-B-i-9), writes that this was "Gertrude's favorite" *Three Lives* review. Mellow quotes it in his book, and John Malcolm Brinnin quotes a representative portion of it in *Third Rose* (I-B-i-2). Because it seems to be one of the first reviews of a work by Stein, and because it is difficult to obtain, the complete text follows:

"Three Lives" by Gertrude Stein, is fiction which no one who reads it can ever forget, but a book for a strictly limited audience. The three lives are "The Good Anna," "The Gentle Lena," and "Melanctha." The good Anna was Miss Mathilda's housekeeper. The gentle Lena, when she had been in this country long enough to know the English, married the good son of German parents. Melanctha is a colored girl, her lover the very best type evolved in the race, a young physician. In this remarkable book one watches humanity groping in the mists of existence. As character study one can speak of it only in superlatives. The originality of its narrative form is as notable. As these humble human lives are groping in bewilderment so does the story telling itself. Not written in the vernacular, it yet gives that impression. At first one fancies the author using repetition as a refrain is used in poetry. But it is something more subtle still; something involved, something turning back, for a new beginning, for a lost strand in the spinning. It makes of the book a very masterpiece of realism, for the reader never escapes from the atmosphere of those lives, so subtly is the incantation wrought into these seeming simple pages. Here is a literary artist of such originality that it is not easy to conjecture what special influences have gone

into the making of her. But the indwelling spirit of it all is a
sweet enlightened sympathy, an unsleeping sense of humor,
and an exquisite carefulness in detail. But it is tautology to
praise Miss Stein's work for this quality or that. Enough
has surely been said to call the attention of those who will
value her work to this new and original artist come into the
field of fiction.

Mellow notes that this review is included in Stein's "notebook
of clippings at Yale." He also lists and quotes from four other
reviews, all published in 1910, of *Three Lives*.

2. Anon. *"Three Lives."* *Nation*, 90 (20 January 1910), 65.

"These stories of the Good Anna, Melanctha, and the
Gentle Lena have a quite extraordinary vitality conveyed in a
most eccentric and difficult form. The gropings of three humble
souls wittingly or unwittingly at odds with life. Whoever can
adjust himself to the repetitions, false starts, and
general circularity of the manner will find himself very near
real people. Too near, possibly. The present writer had an
uncomfortable sense of being immured with a girl wife, a
spinster, and a woman who is neither, between imprisoning
walls which echoed exactly all thoughts and feelings. These
stories utterly lack construction and focus, but give that sense
of urgent life which one gets more commonly in Russian
literature than elsewhere. How the Good Anna spent herself
barrenly for everybody in reach, the Gentle Lena for the notion
of motherhood, while the mulattress Melanctha perished partly
of her own excess of temperament, but more from contact
with a life-diminishing prig and emotionally inert surroundings,
readers who are willing to pay a stiff entrance fee in patient
attention may learn for themselves. From Miss Stein, if she
can consent to clarify her method, much may be expected.
As it is, she writes quite as a Browning escaped from the bonds
of verse might wallow in fiction, only without his antiseptic
whimsicality."

A number of other respectable reviews of *Three
Lives* appeared. They too tend to be in newspapers
that, while major, are not in most libraries. Among
these reviews are the following:

Washington D.C. Herald, 12 December 1909
Boston Morning Herald, 8 January 1910
Philadelphia North American, 8 January 1910
Chicago Record Herald, 22 January 1910
New York City Post, 22 January 1910
Springfield, Massachusetts, Union, 14 August 1910

More reviews appear in 1915 and again in 1927 and
1933.

ii.   Tender Buttons (1914)

1. Rogers, Robert Emmons. "New Outbreaks of Futurism:
   'Tender Buttons,' Curious Experiment of Gertrude
   Stein in Literary Anarchy." *Boston Evening Transcript*,
   11 July 1914, p. 12.

2. Kreymbourg, Alfred. "Gertrude Stein—Hoax and
   Hoaxtress: A Study of the Woman Whose 'Tender
   Buttons' Has Furnished New York with a New Kind
   of Amusement." *The Morning Telegraph*, 7 March 1915,
   p. 6f.

iii.   Geography and Plays (1922)

1. Burke, Kenneth. "Engineering with Words." *Dial*, 74
   (April 1923), 408-12.

2. Van Vechten, Carl. "Medals for Miss Stein." *New York Tribune*, 13 May 1923, Sec. 9, p. 20.

> Van Vechten's *Geography and Plays* review refers to *Making of Americans* as follows: " 'The Making of Americans: Being the History of a Family's Progress' (a work in eight volumes, each containing approximately 500 typewritten pages)."
> Stein is "the founder of the modern movement in English literature"; "Melanctha" influenced several important writers.

3. Pulsifer, Harold T. "Stein Songs and Poetry." *Outlook*, 134 (6 June 1923), 139.

> In *Geography and Plays* "the task [Stein] is attempting . . . is the use of words for the creation of sound patterns without regard to their meanings." Pulsifer suggests Stein experiment instead with a free arrangement of vowels and consonants; readers are less apt to approach such an experiment as subjectively as one with words. Sections of *Geography and Plays* are good poetry although detached from meaning.

4. Sitwell, Edith. "Miss Stein's Stories." *The Nation and the Athenaeum*, 33 (14 July 1923), 492.

> "To sum up the book as far as is possible, I find in it an almost insuperable amount of silliness, an irritating ceaseless rattle like that of American sightseers talking in a boarding-house (this being, I imagine, a deliberate effect), great bravery, a certain real originality, and a few flashes of exquisite beauty. . . ."

5. Sherman, Stuart P. *Points of View*. New York: Scribner's, 1924.

> Chapter 15, "A Note on Gertrude Stein," was originally printed in *Literary Review*, 11 August 1923, p. 891, as "Really Quite Extraordinary." Sherman had read an article by Sherwood Anderson on Stein and wanted to read something by her; this is his reaction to *Geography and Plays*. He quotes Anderson's introduction and goes on to say that Stein's "work . . . though various in theme, form, and style, is of singularly even quality. . . ." Sherman does not accept Anderson's high praise, and writes that a mechanical device would make words more

like "life" than Stein's writings, which give "no glimmer of mind." "I will admit that once or twice it occurred to me faintly that it might just be a joke. But it is impossible to make a joke out of 419 such pages." Sherman also toys with the idea that the book might be a cipher or due to some "mechanical device," but rejects those ideas.

iv.   "An Indian Boy" (1924)

1. Anon. "Fame Contests." *New York Times*, 24 February 1924, Sec. 2, p. 6.
     This contains a positive mention of Stein's poem, which had appeared in *The Reviewer* (Richmond), January 1924.

v.   The Making of Americans (1925; 1934)

1. Moore, Marianne. "The Spare American Emotion." *Dial*, 80 (February 1926), 153-56.

2. Steell, Willis. "An American Novel That Paris Is Talking about." *The Literary Digest International Book Review*, 4 (February 1926), 172-73.

3. Anon. "Gertrude Stein in Critical French Eyes." *Literary Digest*, 88 (6 February 1926), 58-62.
     This contains the same material as covered by the preceding entry.

4. Porter, Katherine Anne. " 'Everybody Is a Real One'." *New York Herald Tribune Books*, 16 January 1927, pp. 1-2.
     Porter's review of *Making of Americans*, "a very necessary book," comments that "this is a deeply American book, and . . . it is a very up-to-date book."

5. Butcher, Fanny. "Book Presents Gertrude Stein As
   She Really Is." *Chicago Daily Tribune*, 10 February
   1934, p. 14.

   Making of Americans is not incomprehensible, but it is also
   "not easy to read." "It has undersenses and oversenses the way
   that notes in music have undertones and overtones."

6. Fadiman, Clifton. Review of *Making of Americans*. *New
   Yorker*, 9 (10 February 1934), 84-87.

7. Fergusson, Francis. "The Making of Gertrude Stein."
   Saturday Review, 10 (17 February 1934), 489.

   The Making of Americans is "oddly moving" and Gertrude
   Stein is "the Benjamin Franklin of the Paris international
   art colony."

8. Aiken, Conrad. "We Ask for Bread." *New Republic*,
   78 (4 April 1934), 219. Reprinted in Conrad Aiken,
   Reviewer's ABC. London: W. H. Allen, 1958.

   A negative criticism of *The Making of Americans*, Aiken's is the
   logical end of B.F. Skinner's "Has Gertrude Stein a Secret?"
   (II-C-30). The Harcourt edition is treated, in three paragraphs, as
   an "automatic" book and the consequence of Stein's automatic
   writings. It contains "tireless and inert repetitiveness
   which becomes as stupefying as it is unintelligible. . . . The
   phrasing is almost completely unsensory, flat and
   colorless. . . ."
      "The book is a complete aesthetic miscalculation: it is
   dull. . . ."

Reviews of the play by Leon Katz have been
published but have little bearing on Stein's work.

vi. Composition As Explanation (1926)

1. Anon. "Composition As Explanation." *New York
   Times*, 24 October 1926, Sec. 2, p. 8.

   This is an editorial on the Dial printing of "Composition As

Explanation." It is a very sarcastic article which
nonetheless speaks of Stein as "one of the most painstaking,
original and creative of contemporary authors." Composition,
however, is "a subject usually the more darkened the more
it is explained."

vii.   Useful Knowledge (1928)

1. Porter, Katherine Anne. "Second Wind." *New York
   Herald Tribune Books*, 23 September 1928, p. 7.

   This is the first appearance of Porter's now famous *Useful
   Knowledge* parody.

2. Wilson, Edmund. "Nonsense." *New Republic*, 58
   (20 February 1929), 21-22.

   Wilson finds most of *Useful Knowledge* "tiresome."
   This review contains a discussion of nonsense and sense in
   literature, "which is not explicable by what we call 'reason',
   or reducible to what we call 'logic'," in order not to create "a
   misleading impression" by calling Stein's book nonsense.

3. Anon. *"Useful Knowledge."* *New Statesman*, 13 April
   1929, p. 22.

   "Miss Stein is dull. She has no word-sense, no skill in
   employing words and images."

4. Anon. Review of *Useful Knowledge*. *London Times Literary
   Supplement*, 25 April 1929, p. 342.

   "Curious gleams of simple humor contorted into a strange
   shape seem at moments to appear in Miss Stein's book," which is
   seen as nonsense, however; Stein "still writes incomprehensibly."

viii.   Lucy Church Amiably (1930)

1. Coates, R.M. Review of *Lucy Church Amiably*. *New
   Yorker*, 8 (20 February 1932, out-of-town issue),
   69-70.

2. Hubbell, Lindley Williams. "The Plain Editions of
   Gertrude Stein." *Contempo*, 25 October 1933, pp. 1
   and 4.
   Stein's work is "the mountain from which two generations
   have quarried for their lesser structures."

See also II-C-17.

ix.   How to Write (1931)

1. Carter, David. "Grammar Takes a Trip." *London
   Times Literary Supplement*, 12 March 1976, p. 284.
   Stein's ideas concerning language are close to those of
   William James and Alfred North Whitehead. "There is an
   enormous amount in this book, but it can be absorbed only a
   fragment at a time because her writing demands that the
   reader postulate a speaker for each sentence, a speaker for
   whom those words would be a way of being in the world, and this
   requires an enormous effort of participation. However this
   was Stein's crusade, to make the effort and reality of language
   visible once more and to ground it in individual and cultural
   perspectives on life."

x.   G.M.P. (1933)

xi.   The Autobiography of Alice B. Toklas (1933)

1. Flanner, Janet (Genêt). Review of *Autobiography of
   Alice B. Toklas. New Yorker*, 9 (4 May 1933), 37.
   Reprinted in *Paris Was Yesterday (1925-1939)*.

2. Van Doren, Carl. Review of *The Autobiography of Alice
   B. Toklas. Wings*, September 1933, pp. 5-7.

3. Butcher, Fanny. "Gertrude Stein Writes a Book in Simple Style." *Chicago Daily Tribune*, 2 September 1933, p. 8.

> Butcher synopsizes *The Autobiography*. Among her more quotable quotes are: "There is in Europe today no single person who has been of more influence in the modern arts than Gertrude Stein"; "No person with any feel at all for modern American literature has missed 'Three Lives'."
> Fanny Butcher "made a pilgrimage to Belignin."

4. Fadiman, Clifton. Review of *The Autobiography of Alice B. Toklas. New Yorker*, 9 (2 September 1933), 50-51.

5. Bromfield, Louis. "Gertrude Stein, Experimenter with Words." *New York Herald Tribune*, 3 September 1933, Sec. 7, pp. 1-2.

> "A great part of the excitement of the book comes from the ability of Gertrude Stein to make the cook, the occasional passerby, the tenant across the court, the policeman, as vivid and as fascinating as any of the personable, gifted and celebrated figures of whom she writes. . . ." Bromfield raves about Stein, and then writes about her presence in the *Autobiography*, which was an "historical event in American writing."

6. Kingsbury, Edward M. "Gertrude Stein Articulates at Last." *New York Times*, 3 September 1933, Sec. 5, p. 2.

> The *Autobiography* is the "record of a rich, vivid and various experience. It is not without its wit and malice. . . . The repetitive and some other distinctions of Gertrude Stein's manner and method are infrequent."

7. Troy, William. "A Note on Gertrude Stein." *Nation*, 137 (6 September 1933), 274-75.

> " . . . among books of literary reminiscences Miss Stein's is one of the richest, wittiest, and most irreverent ever written. . . ." The book gives insight "into the genesis

of the mind and sensibility reflected in Gertrude Stein's other
and more characteristic books."

Troy asks two questions: what has Stein been attempting;
what is the value of her work. The first question deals "not
only with her method, style and processes of composition but
also with her view or 'vision' of experience." The second
deals with evaluation, and depends in part on the answer to
the first question.

Stein, in common with other American writers, has "an
orientation from experience toward the abstract, an orientation
that has been so continuous as to constitute a tradition,
if not actually *the* American tradition."

8. RP. "In Tender Slippers." *Christian Science Monitor*,
   9 September 1933, p. 6.

9. Agee, James. "Stein's Way." *Time*, 22 (11 September
   1933), 57-60.

   A typical *Time* review, more summary than review.

10. Knickerbocker, William S. "Stunning Stein."
    Sewanee Review, 41 (October-December 1933),
    498-99.

    In this parody of Stein's style (supposedly a review of
    Autobiography), Knickerbocker ends by comparing Stein
    with the Emperor's New Clothes.

11. IMP. "Turns with a Bookworm." *New York Herald
    Tribune*, 1 October 1933, Sec. 7, p. 19.

    In a one-paragraph mention, IMP manages to equate Stein
    with an egotist with a baby. "If a baby could write a book it
    would resemble 'The Autobiography of Alice B. Toklas'."

12. Wilson, Edmund. "27 rue de Fleurus." *New Republic*,
    76 (11 October 1933), 246-47. Reprinted in Edmund
    Wilson, *The Shores of Light: A Literary Chronicle of the
    Twenties and Thirties*. New York: Farrar, Straus, and
    Young, 1952.

    Stein's criticisms in *Autobiography* are affected by the fact
    that "she is the ruler of a salon" and "is also herself a writer

who has had a very hard time to get published and who has
never yet had the recognition to which she considers herself
entitled." Alice B. Toklas has been created as an individual
distinguishable from Gertrude Stein. The chapters after Guillaume
Apollinaire's death are not as exciting as those before the
war.

13. Anon. "Memoirs by Proxy." *Spectator* (London),
    151 (13 October 1933), 496.

   The *Autobiography* "is written with extreme simplicity: it
is neither a development of Miss Stein's recent pattern-making
nor a reversion to the very interesting manner of *Three
Lives*: it is a direct narrative of actual events, there is no
attempt at portrayal of character except in so far as the style
is intended to express a rather childlike and easily-impressed
mentality, and there is no comment on that fantastic life of
which Miss Toklas and Miss Stein were privileged spectators."

14. ———. "Integer Vitae." *New Statesman and Nation*,
    14 October 1933, pp. 450 and 452.

   The *Autobiography* is "a perfect piece of narration,"
"delightful, and brilliant with sincerity." Stein has "a knack
for getting at the quiddity of friends and acquaintances."

15. ———. "Miss Gertrude Stein." *London Times Literary
    Supplement*, 9 November 1933, p. 767.

16. Chew, Samuel S. "O Heart, Rise Not up against Me
    As a Witness." *Yale Review*, 23 (Winter 1934), 392-97.

   Chew's article contains a review in which appear trivialities,
worship, and so on. "Actually, the 'Autobiography' is a very
entertaining book, too long, too generously inclusive of
all the people who, Miss Stein thinks, are . . . entitled to
admission . . . ; too anecdotic and too chaotic; but
valuable for its vivid characterization of notable people and
for its equally vivid picture of a 'movement', a 'period', a
'moment' in the world of genuinely creative art, seen from
the vantage point of its very centre."

17. Nelson, John Herbert. Review of *The Autobiography of Alice B. Toklas*. *American Literature*, 5 (January 1934), 392-94.

> Stein "is a witty woman, a clever commentator on life, a skillful wielder of satire; and she has the ability of going straight to the heart of a matter, of making an explanation in the clearest, most pointed terms," but she gives here no "elementary elucidation" of her works.

xii.   Four Saints in Three Acts (1934)

1. Van Vechten, Carl. "A Few Notes about *Four Saints in Three Acts*." *Four Saints in Three Acts: An Opera to Be Sung*, by Gertrude Stein. New York: Random House, 1934.

> In this article, dated 8 February 1934, Van Vechten writes: "It becomes more and more evident to me that if appreciation of the text of Miss Stein is not instinctive with a person he never acquires it." He also mentions that there was a Picasso show in the same building as *Four Saints*.

2. H. H. "Four Saints' Acts Is Acts in 30 Acts." *New York Times*, 9 February 1934, p. 22.

> This review gives all the particulars—cast, director, set designer—of the first performance (in Hartford).

3. Rosenfeld, Paul. "Prepare for Saints!" *New Republic*, 78 (21 February 1934), 48.

4. Burke, Kenneth. "Two Brands of Piety." *Nation*, 138 (28 February 1934), 256-58.

> "The Stein-Thomson number had about it much of the alembication, the archness and mild effrontery that has regularly gone with the Parisian cosmopolitanism of our cultural expatriates. Its seriousness was frequently overlaid with the apologetic smirks of fashion." Her "extremely loquacious reticence shows evidence of a waking deliberation which too

often makes her lines elusive rather than allusive," and her "nonsense, as reinforced by Thomson, has established its great musicality."

5. Stevens, George. "Syllabus of Syllables." *Saturday Review*, 10 (3 March 1934), 519.

   A half-column of parody.

6. Young, Stark. "One Moment Alit." *New Republic*, 78 (7 March 1934), 105.

7. Skinner, Richard Dana. "The Play: *Four Saints in Three Acts.*" *Commonweal*, 19 (9 March 1934), 525.

   Skinner writes of "the cryptograms of Gertrude Stein's alleged prose." Thomson's music, Florine Stettheimer and Kate Drain Lawson are approved of, but Stein is "precious," and neither she nor her opera are okay.

8. Canby, Henry Seidel. "Dressmakers for Art." *Saturday Review*, 10 (24 March 1934), 572.

   Canby relates how the opera was greeted. Mr. Canby is neither overcome with sentimental nostalgia (as is Sherwood Anderson) nor is he overcome by obtuse sarcasm; his criticisms, both positive and negative, are as objective as criticism can be without totally annihilating the subjective opinion of the critic.

9. Krutch, Joseph Wood. "A Prepare for Saints." *Nation*, 138 (4 April 1934), 396 and 398.

   " 'Four Saints in Three Acts' is a success because all its elements . . . go so well with one another while remaining totally irrelevant to life, logic, or common sense."

10. Young, Stark. "Might It Be Mountains?" *New Republic*, 78 (11 April 1934), 246.

11. Rosenfeld, Paul. *Discoveries of a Music Critic.* New York: Harcourt, Brace, 1936.

    Included in his review of *Four Saints* is a good description of the stage setting, and of the way the opera moved—action, music, blacks, costumes. The opera left "more than one spectator sorry he possessed more than an ocular sense. The eye had been amused by Florine Stettheimer's elfish half jewel-box, half candy-box set and costumes. But the ear had been exposed to a vacuum utterly empty of tension and ideas and musical quality and containing somebody being tediously 'gay'."

Four Saints is "a thirty-minute vaudeville stunt stretched out to the length of eighteen saints in four acts and two and a half hours." The two ideas which seem to make up the opera are concerned: 1) with the masculine and feminine "essences" in the "Spanish landscape"; 2) with the relationship of the saints to the Catholic religion.

12. Watt, Douglas. "Opera in English." *New Yorker,* 28 (26 April 1952), 122-24.

Four Saints is "a kind of sublime minstrel show," and "one of the few operas ever written in which the librettist's name has figured as prominently as the composer's."

13. Anon. "Not Four—Thirty Six." *Newsweek,* 39 (28 April 1952), 52.

14. Haggin, B. H. "Music." *Nation,* 174 (3 May 1952), 437-38.

15. Kolodin, Irving. "A Week of Thomson, Honegger, Szymanowski, and Berg." *Saturday Review,* 35 (3 May 1952), 33.

"What was the singular strength of 'Four Saints' twenty years ago—its modernity'—is now its heavy dragging weight."

16. Nathan, George Jean. "The Grass Menagerie— Musicalized Fog." *Theatre Arts,* 36 (June 1952), 19.

Nathan is prejudiced against Stein because of her unintelligibility; Thomson's music is "imaginative, ingenious and here and there witty."

17. Beyer, William. "The State of the Theatre: Modern

Dance and Opera." *School and Society,* 75 (21 June
1952), 393-94.

> Stein's libretto is "totally irrelevant but nonetheless
> gay gobble-de-gook" and "Stein's stammerings." Beyer tends,
> however, towards a positive view, and includes information on
> Thomson's score for this "singularly American and definitely
> modern" opera.

18. Hayes, R. "Making of Americans." *Commonweal,* 64
    (28 September 1956), 634-35.

> "The mastering theme of Miss Stein's work, one sees at
> this remove, was the definition of *identity.* . . ."

19. Ericson, Raymond. " 'Four Saints' to Take a New
    Trip." *New York Times,* 26 April 1970, Sec. 2, p. 19.

> The announcement of another revival of *Four Saints.*

xiii.   Portraits and Prayers (1934)

1. Canby, Henry Seidel. "Cheating at Solitaire." *Saturday
   Review,* 11 (17 November 1934), 290. Reprinted in
   Henry Seidel Canby, *Seven Years Harvest: Notes on
   Contemporary Literature.* New York: Farrar and
   Rinehart, 1936.

> Although Canby has not read *Portraits and Prayers,* he makes
> some very interesting positive and negative remarks about
> Stein and her work. Among other things, he praises her for
> having a good ear, which is "hindered by her unfortunate
> predilection for words." All in all, Canby is logical in his
> criticisms and, although negative, not sarcastic.

2. Fadiman, Clifton. Review of *Portraits and Prayers. New
   Yorker,* 10 (17 November 1934, out-of-town issue), 86.

3. Anon. "But a Stein Is a Stein Is a Stein." *New York
   Times,* 18 November 1934, Sec. 5, p. 10.

> "There is nothing in this book to merit more than five

minutes' attention of a reasonably honest and intelligent mind."
The reviewer does allow that Stein taught Ernest Hemingway,
Sherwood Anderson and others "the value of repetition, of the
short sentence, of the sparing use of adjectives," but asks why
we should treat "as a twentieth-century revelation" "three of the
oldest devices known to rhetoric."

4. Alsop, Joseph, Jr. "In Words Gertrude Stein Finds
   Emotions." *New York Herald Tribune*, 94 (25 November
   1934), Sec. 7, 5.

   Alsop "found hardly a comprehensible paragraph in all of
   'Portraits and Prayers'." But, considering Stein's personality
   and his own impression of *Three Lives*, he went to Miss
   Stein—in New York at the beginning of her American
   trip—for an explanation.
   "Possibly the trouble lies in Miss Stein's abnormal
   sensitivity to words and arrangements of words." The
   trouble, that is, is that Stein has "misapprehended the very
   nature of words." Nonetheless "the portraits . . . are
   exceedingly pleasant to read aloud, for Miss Stein's distinguished
   sense of verbal rhythm gives even the most startling of them
   a curious musical quality." Stein's "change of style" is the
   "major tragedy of modern literature."

5. Wilson, Edmund. "One Being Musing Dosing." *New
   Republic*, 81 (26 December 1934), 198.

   "The pieces are considerably varied and make a representative
   selection of Miss Stein's work. They range from the simple
   and engaging to the exasperating and opaque."
   "There is nothing new to say about Miss Stein. She is a
   first-rate literary talent to whom something very strange and
   probably unfortunate has happened—perhaps it is the basic
   emptiness of the life of the artistic foreigner in Paris."

xiv.   Lectures in America (1935)

1. Strauss, Harold. "Miss Stein's Lectures." *New York
   Times*, 14 April 1935, Sec. 6, p. 12.

   Strauss doesn't like *Lectures in America* or Stein's theories.

"Her esthetics is any device which by its incomprehensibility maintains the ivory tower of her uniqueness."

2. Burke, Kenneth. "The Impartial Essence." *New Republic*, 83 (3 July 1935), 227.

"As it stands, I maintain that it is (a) the first draft of a critical credo, (b) complicated by the copresence of its revision, (c) further vitiated by the fact that the revisionary process was not applied to all its parts. Above all, I believe, a complete revision would require her to stress (at least in this 'imperfect world' of history) the *dramatic*, the *active*, the *partisan*, in direct contrast with the feature of *passivity* that is now infused through her doctrine of portrait and essence."

xv. Narration (1935)

1. Canby, Henry Seidel. "Belles Lettres." *Saturday Review*, 13 (21 December 1935), 18.

Narration contains "a good deal of shrewd common sense— for those who know how to get it out."

2. Davies, Hugh Sykes. "*Narration* by Gertrude Stein." *Criterion*, 15 (July 1936), 752-55.

This is a criticism of four lectures (now printed and bound as *Narration*) delivered at the University of Chicago. Davies's main criticisms are loose thinking, bad criticism, lack of punctuation: "punctuated or unpunctuated her sentences are simply bad, ill-constructed, confused and rhythmless."

Her mannerisms (repetition, lack of facts or illustrations) are not adaptable for giving lectures, i.e. making serious statements.

xvi. The Geographical History of America Or The Relation of Human Nature to the Human Mind (1936)

1. Alsop, Joseph, Jr. "Gertrude Stein on Writing:

Behind Her Queer Verbal Music Is a Sharp
Distinction between Human Mind and Human
Nature." *New York Herald Tribune*, 96 (10 January
1937), Sec. 10, 2.

In what is primarily a review of *The Geographical History of
America*, Alsop also writes that *Three Lives* is "her sufficient ticket
of admission to the small company of writers of the last decades
who have something to say and know how to say it. . . . "
Although Alsop does say that *Geographical History* "is a long
and a minute study of the creative process, full of much that is
rewarding, and much that is horribly puzzling," the review is
mostly an attempt at synopsis. Alsop feels that the defect
in Stein's literary theories lies in her "very denial of the
problem of communication."

"Her book is a fascinating one since the thesis it expresses
is her reason for departure from the common literary forms.
It is full of her peculiar dry wit, and her queer verbal music,
which she composes by using words as pure sound. . . . There
is much that is shrewd in it. . . ."

Alsop expresses sorrow that Stein changed her style from
that of *Three Lives* to that of *Geographical History*.

xvii.   Everybody's Autobiography (1937)

1. Fadiman, Clifton. "Genius Self-Revealed." *New
   Yorker*, 13 (4 December 1937, out-of-town issue),
   115-18.

   Mr. Harvey Eagleson (II-C-47) stated that "most reviewers,
   like Clifton Fadiman in *The New Yorker*, took the publication of
   her book as an occasion for making 'wise-cracking' remarks
   at her expense."

2. Rascoe, Burton. "Self-Confidential." *Saturday Review*,
   17 (4 December 1937), 11 and 56.

   This is a nonreview: Rascoe had a visiting houseboy,
   Hashimura Togo, read the book and write what he thought
   about it.

3. Jack, Peter Munro. "Gertrude Stein Continues the Story of Her Life." *New York Times,* 5 December 1937, Sec. 7, p. 7.

> *Everybody's Autobiography* is "commentary rather than creation." "Miss Stein's chief asset in writing is her colossal egotism, and her chief deficiency is her inability to create character." Jack's complaints about the book are that "the explanations and explorations that we might have hoped for are not there."

4. Butcher, Fanny. "Three Unusual Women Live in These Volumes." *Chicago Daily Tribune,* 11 December 1937, p. 15.

> Butcher reviews Amelia Earhart's *Last Flight,* Sackville-West's *Pepita,* and Stein's *Everybody's Autobiography,* which "must be read slowly, for it leaps, in the same sentence, through time and space. . . ."

5. Barry, Iris. "Gertrude Stein Came Home." *New York Herald Tribune,* 12 December 1937, Sec. 10, p. 6.

6. Lewis, Sinclair. "The Gas Goddess." *Newsweek,* 10 (13 December 1937), 36.

xviii. Picasso (1938)

1. Anon. "Miss Stein on Picasso." *London Times Literary Supplement,* 26 November 1938, p. 751.

> *Picasso* is a "straightforward" book. "It is for such first-hand information, and for a number of lighter and amusing anecdotes, that the average reader will go to this book." The reviewer blames Stein's style on Picasso's influence.

2. Hinks, Roger. "Profile of Picasso." *Spectator* (London), 162 (17 February 1939), 271-72.

> *Picasso* is "a curiously attractive, yet at the same time most unsatisfactory essay." "What prevents Miss Stein and Picasso

from being geniuses, in spite of all their originality, is their
fatal propensity to complicate things in a new way when they
do not feel up to seeing things with 'another vision than that
of all the world'."

3. Fadiman, Clifton. "Mixed Bag." *New Yorker*, 15
   (18 February 1939, out-of-town issue), 68-69.

   As long as Stein's subject is not Stein, Stein can be
   "informative and even acute."

4. Gorman, Herbert. "A Picasso Is a Picasso Is a —."
   New York Times, 5 March 1939, Sec. 6, p. 9.

   Stein's style, in *Picasso*, is "contagious." She "offers one of
   the few intelligent explanations of cubism that have ever been
   written."

5. ECS. "Pablo, According to Gertrude." *Christian
   Science Monitor Weekly Magazine Section*, 11 March
   1939, p. 11.

   In *Picasso*, Stein's "style has the air of having been dictated
   but not read, or at least not revised. . . . Her style is logical,
   assuming that individuality of experience may find
   individuality of expression."

6. Mongan, Agnes. "Stein on Picasso." *Saturday Review*,
   19 (18 March 1939), 11.

   In *Picasso* "few of [Stein's] familiar mannerisms are lacking,
   but there is more punctuation and less repetition than
   formerly."

7. Swan, Natalie. "Stein on Picasso." *New Republic*,
   99 (5 July 1939), 259.

   Picasso is "a polite and charming illustrated lecture." "Miss
   Stein's observations are witty and often illuminating; more
   illuminating perhaps in regard to her own work than to the work
   of her star performer." She is unable to explain adequately
   Picasso's "place in society."

xix. Prothalamium for Bobolink and His Louise (1939)

See II-C-155.

xx. The World Is Round (1939)

1. Bechtel, Louise Seaman. "Gertrude Stein for
   Children." *Horn Book*, 15 (September 1939), 286-91.
   Reprinted in Louise Seaman Bechtel, *Books in Search
   of Children: Speeches and Essays*. London: Hamish
   Hamilton, 1970.

   The first half of Bechtel's review seems to be written for
   children. *World Is Round* is "an unforgettable creative
   experience"; "for me, this is the first time that her style
   has spoken truly and artistically as perfectly fitted to her
   thought."
   "Miss Stein is not tops even in her own field; she cannot
   touch the Joyce of *Ulysses*, for instance, or Virginia Woolf. But
   she is one freeing agent who was peculiarly fitted to do her
   good piece for modern children."

2. Becker, May Lamberton. "Books for Young People."
   New York Herald Tribune, 24 September 1939, Sec. 9,
   p. 6.

   "Pure delight, simple pleasure, is what little children will
   get as they listen, a chapter or so at a time, to 'The World
   Is Round'. So will the adult who reads it to them, unless his
   mind is too stiff to bend with the rhythm."

3. Mackenzie, Catherine. "Children and Parents." *New
   York Times*, 24 September 1939, Sec. 2, p. 8.

   Mackenzie writes about the sound of words and children's
   enjoyment of the aural.

4. Buell, Ellen Lewis. "By Gertrude Stein." *New York Times*, 12 November 1939, Sec. 6, pp. 10 and 20.

> Stein has at last found her audience. Buell speaks of the book's delightfulness for children and its nostalgic quality for adults.

5. Benét, Rosemary Carr. "The Children's Bookshop: Some of the Highlights." *Saturday Review*, 21 (18 November 1939), 22.

> " 'It jabber-jabbers'."

6. Fadiman, Clifton. "The Children's Harvest." *New Yorker*, 15 (25 November 1939, out-of-town issue), 72.

> *The World Is Round* is "buried in tedious mannerisms and lumbering whimsy."

7. Baker, Gilbert. "A Boy Decides." *New Statesman and Nation*, 18 (16 December 1939), 901 and 904.

> One of the three books reviewed by Baker, an eight-year-old, is *World Is Round*. He feels "it would be best for a learning rather than a reading book because of the rhymes" and realizes "it's not very good for reading to oneself."

8. Wilson, Edmund and Chauncey Hackett. "Slightly Pied Pipers." *New Republic*, 101 (20 December 1939), 266-67.

> Wilson and Hackett review *The World Is Round* and T.S. Eliot's *Old Possum's Book of Practical Cats*. Wilson thinks that the "tendency" of " 'difficult' writers to go in for children's books" might mean "that they evidently do not feel at the moment that they have anything better to do."
>
> Hackett writes that *The World Is Round* is "a delicious confection of a book, printed in dark blue on rose-colored paper. The simplicity of the diction is extreme."

xxi.   Paris France (1940)

1. Anon. "France: A True Picture in Terms of Stein."
   London Times Literary Supplement, 25 May 1940, p. 252.

   This is a very favorable short article—not really a
   criticism—on *Paris France*. "Her style, so crystal clear that
   a child of seven could understand it, paints a picture of
   France correct to the smallest detail." *Despite* her disregard
   of punctuation, says the reviewer, "the value of her insight
   remains and her integrity is untouched."

2. Flanner, Janet (Genêt). "History Tramps down the
   Champs Elysses." *New York Times*, 23 June 1940,
   Sec. 9, p. 1.

   This review was written after "Germany's march through
   Western Europe"; Flanner therefore sees the book as a
   celebration of "the France which was, until a month ago."
   Paris France contains "the essential specialities of French
   civilized life."

3. Woods, Katherine. "Civilization and the French."
   New York Times, 23 June 1940, Sec. 6, pp. 1 and 13.

   Paris France is "a happy book about France," and Stein is
   "the communication of the sense of France."

4. Stearns, Harold E. "Gertrude Stein's France."
   Saturday Review, 22 (13 July 1940), 6.

   "For once Miss Stein is concise, forthright, clear, and
   articulate." The subject has dominated Stein's verbal
   experimentation in this book.

5. Chamberlain, Dorothy. "Her France, Her Paris."
   New Republic, 103 (22 July 1940), 123-24.

   Paris France is about Stein's Paris, Stein's France, "not
   theirs" (the French). "For its literary quality, for its nostalgic
   pictures of life in France, and for the lesson to be learned

from the fallacies of an intellectual class and the weaknesses that democracy has tolerated, 'Paris France' is a book you should read." Chamberlain takes some quotations completely out of context and misreads them.

6. O'Brien, Justin. "Miss Stein and France." *Nation*, 151 (27 July 1940), 76.

"With all its charms and flavor and superficiality, 'Paris France' is a pathetic little book."

7. Brégy, Katherine. *"Paris France."* *Commonweal*, 32 (23 August 1940), 373.

It is "the most stimulating book Miss Stein has given us," although "a few superficial eccentricities of style remain. . . ."

8. Barry, Joseph. *"Paris France* Reviewed." *Widening Circle*, 1, No. 4 (1973), 3-5.

9. Kesting, Marianne. "Sie war die Mutter der Moderne: Selbstbekenntnisse von Gertrude Stein." *Die Zeit*, 23 January 1976, p. 38.

Kesting reviews *"Paris Frankreich."* In her attempt to criticize Stein's *Paris France*, Kesting overlooks the major objection to the 1975 publication in Frankfurt: *Paris Frankreich* is the German translation of the French translation of Stein's *Paris France*.

xxii. What Are Masterpieces (1940)

1. Fadiman, Clifton. "Books." *New Yorker*, 16 (19 October 1940), 87.

"At this late date there is very little to say about Miss Stein, and Miss Stein will say it."

xxiii. Ida, a Novel (1941)

1. Fadiman, Clifton. "Getting Gertie's Ida." *New Yorker*, 17 (15 February 1941, out-of-town issue), 78.

   Stein "has set herself to solve, and has succeeded in solving, the most difficult problem in prose composition—to write something that will not arrest the attention in any way, manner, shape, or form."

2. Hauser, Marianne. "Miss Stein's Ida." *New York Times*, 16 February 1941, Sec. 6, p. 7.

   "One might call [*Ida*] a short novel, a long poem or a modern fairy tale; or a painting in words, reminding of a Dali rather than of a Picasso." Hauser gives the plot, and then comments that *Ida* "is a curious little book, too thin, too deliberate to be called crazy, and too well done to be laughed off." The happiest parts of the book are Stein's humor.

3. Anon. "Abstract Prose." *Time*, 37 (17 February 1941), 99-100.

   The reviewer outlines the story. Although the article is inadequate, the following suggestions (cf. Eagleson, II-C-47) are contained: "Read it with care, but require no sense of it that it does not yield. Read it aloud. Read it as poetry must be read or music listened to: several times. Read it for pleasure only. If it displeases you, quit."

4. Auden, W.H. "All about Ida." *Saturday Review*, 23 (22 February 1941), 8.

   This is subtitled "Simplified by W.H. Auden," and pretends to be *Ida*.

5. Chamberlain, Dorothy. "Gertrude Stein, Amiably." *New Republic*, 104 (7 April 1941), 477.

   This is an interesting article, but it adds nothing to the study of either Stein or her literature, especially *Ida*, which Chamberlain here purports to review.

xxiv.   Wars I Have Seen (1945)

1. Hackett, Francis. *On Judging Books: In General and Particular*. New York: John Day Co., 1947.

   The New York Times (11 March 1945) review is reprinted here.

2. Redman, Ben Ray. "The Importance of Being Earnest." *Saturday Review*, 28 (10 March 1945), 8 and 30.

   Despite rhymes, rhythms and lack of punctuation, Redman writes "Miss Stein could not have said just what she had to say, as effectively as she has said it, without these rhythms, or without the repetitions she loves." Her prose is "a mature, flexible, wonderfully useful instrument," and her "great virtue" is "her simplicity, her amazing, utter simplicity. . . ."

3. Cowley, Malcolm. "Gertrude Stein for the Plain Reader." *New York Times*, 11 March 1945, Sec. 7, pp. 1 and 22.

   Wars is a good book because Stein forgets for a while about herself. Everything is "reduced to a village scale."

   "On second reading the 'autobiography' is a disappointing book." Cowley asks how someone so influential in literature, so famous as a conversationalist, could have written so many dull books.

4. Wilson, Edmund. Review of *Wars I Have Seen*. *New Yorker*, 21 (17 March 1945), 91-92.

5. Wahl, Jean. "Miss Stein's Battle." *New Republic*, 112 (19 March 1945), 396-98.

   Wahl takes a fine-tooth comb to *Wars*—and to the recent armistice—and finds much she does not like. She attacks Stein's logic. On the other hand, Wahl does not seem to dislike the book; she is basically trying to correct "the great things that are wrong"—political statements—in *Wars*.

6. Weeks, Edward. "The Atlantic Bookshelf: The Peripatetic Reviewer." *Atlantic Monthly*, 175 (April 1945), 127-33.

   "A Woman Preoccupied" reviews *Wars*.

7. Anon. "From 'Business English' to Gertrude Stein." *Saturday Evening Post*, 217 (12 May 1945), 112.

   In a brief mention the reviewer compares Stein's style to written records of testimonies before investigating committees.

8. Benedict, Libby. "The Disillusionment That Calls Itself Objectivity." *New York Times*, 20 May 1945, Sec. 7, p. 4.

   An antiwar, antifascism article, based on a misunderstanding and misapprehension of Stein and her work, this review goes on to criticize "irresponsible cynicism" on the part of Stein and other writers.

   At the time this article was written, Miss Benedict was "employed in the features division of the News and Features Bureau of the Affairs of War Information."

xxv.   Brewsie and Willie (1946)

1. Sulzberger, C.L. "GI Novel Written by Gertrude Stein." *New York Times*, 25 August 1945, p. 13.

   An interview concerned with the writing of *Brewsie and Willie*.

2. Wilson, Edmund. Review of *Brewsie and Willie*. *New Yorker*, 22 (15 June 1946), 92-93.

3. Cowley, Malcolm. "American Patriot by Remote Control." *New York Herald Tribune*, 21 July 1946, Sec. 7, p. 5.

   Cowley states that he cannot believe that it is Stein who

is one of the first to say things that must be said à propos consumption, economy, isolationism.
"She writes conversation pieces."

4. Poore, Charles. "GI Conversation Piece, Translated into the Steinese." *New York Times*, 21 July 1946, Sec. 7, p. 7.

One should start with the last chapter first. "In a world filled with the double talk of the politicians, the economists and the scientists, [Stein's style] sounds saner and saner every day."

5. Woodburn, John. "Words in Their Meaning." *Saturday Review*, 29 (27 July 1946), 13.

Brewsie and Willie is a "good little colloquial book."
Stein is "a good writer of plain words which have been called incomprehensible by too many of her fellow-Americans, the ones who have considered her not so much sensible and interesting, which she is, as pretentious and dull, which they are."
"She has also been charged with taking words out of their meaning and converting them to her own use, which is incompetent criticism, inasmuch as Miss Stein has always effected her writing by using the English language exactly and respectfully, refusing to dilute the simple primary colors of the words."

6. Paulding, C.G. "Let Them Talk and Talk." *Commonweal*, 44 (2 August 1946), 384-85.

"It has become at last possible to write about a book by Gertrude Stein because nobody in his senses thinks any more that she is a joke." Two difficulties with the book are the "discipline of her cadences" and the characters who "talk and talk."

7. Warshow, Robert S. " 'Gerty' and the G.I.'s." *Nation*, 163 (5 October 1946), 383-84.

xxvi. Four in America (1947)

1. Anon. "Not for the Tired." *Time*, 50 (17 November 1947), 113-14.

   The reviewer is grateful for Thornton Wilder's introduction and is critical of Stein for her lethargic development of points. "Gertrude Stein had leisure, intelligence, curiosity and quite a bit of gall."

2. Watts, Richard, Jr. "Writing Out Loud." *New Republic*, 117 (17 November 1947), 28.

   "Save for the addicts, this is a dull and exasperating book. . . ."

3. Gray, James. "Competent Priestess." *Saturday Review*, 30 (22 November 1947), 30-31.

   The basic idea of *Four in America* is that "the creative process is impelled by the same kind of power no matter what may be its manifestation."
   "In each of Gertrude Stein's work, it is easy, if one is willing to be patient and trusting, to find the theme, to follow all the variations on it, to discover with pleasure how she plays upon it, modifies it, elaborates it, achieves teasing, provocative, amusing effects with it. And then it becomes easier still to discover her in the ingenious act of introducing a second theme to support the first, to carry on little duels and conversations with it so that, in the end, her follower is refreshed by a belief in the honesty and the importance of what she is about." " 'Listen' is the key word of these essays."

4. Sloper, L.A. "Nonsense." *Christian Science Monitor Magazine Section*, 22 November 1947, p. 17.

   This five-paragraph review is rather a taken-for-granted put down of Stein, and of Thornton Wilder for writing an introduction to the book. ". . . in an age when the human race seems bent on its own destruction [.] [We] have more important things on our minds than toying with literary affectations."

5. Fitts, Dudley. "Toasted Susie Is My Ice-Cream." *New York Times*, 30 November 1947, Sec. 7, p. 5.

> "The sincere work of a consummate artist and profound intelligence, [*Four in America*] is a book for the youthful minds of people young and old who are eager to investigate what lies around the corner."

6. Morris, Lloyd. "Gertrude Stein's Method." *New York Herald Tribune*, 30 November 1947, Sec. 7, p. 19.

> In what is supposedly a review of *Four in America*, Morris remarks that "it was [Stein's] happy discovery that rumination could be made a literary method. The consequences for contemporary writing are still to be estimated."

7. Fremantle, Anne. "Expatriate's End." *Commonweal*, 47 (12 December 1947), 229-30.

xxvii.   Mother of Us All (Listed here by performance date, 1947; it was first printed in **Last Operas and Plays**, 1949.)

1. Simon, Robert A. "Musical Events." *New Yorker*, 23 (17 May 1947), 103-04.

> *Mother of Us All* was an excellent idea which "resulted in an original, entertaining, and provocative libretto."

2. Phelan, Kappo. "Stage and Screen." *Commonweal*, 46 (30 May 1947), 167-68.

> "As there is no machinery of logic at work—no plot—but more, a series of interlocking sequential vignettes, one finds that meaning, wisdom, and action in the piece are cumulative rather than immediately established. However . . . *character* throughout is not only cumulative but also immediate."
> Stein is "American . . . the Laughing American."

3. Haggin, B.H. "Music." *Nation*, 164 (31 May 1947), 667.

4. Smith, Cecil. "Sounds of Spring." *New Republic*,
   116 (2 June 1947), 33.

> *Mother of Us All* has touching moments as well as meaning.

5. ———. "Gertrude S., Virgil T., and Susan B."
   Theatre Arts, 31 (July 1947), 17-18.

> *Mother of Us All* is not an equal of *Four Saints in Three Acts*.
> The libretto is "thoughtful, patriotic, compassionate, stern and
> witty."

6. Beyer, William. "The State of the Theater: Drama
   and Music Drama." *School and Society*, 66 (26 July
   1947), 67.

> *Mother of Us All* is a "political fantasy" and "provides another
> evening of delightful nonsense, both musically and verbally."

7. Henahan, Donal. "Thomson and Stein in Revival."
   New York Times, 2 August 1971, p. 2.

> The opera is a women's lib work and was well ahead of its time.

See also II-E-xii-18.

This is only a sampling of opera reviews. The recent
Santa Fe production and recording with Robert
Indiana's scenery and costumes has been reviewed
a number of times; as with most reviews listed here,
even the recent ones have more to do with production
than with Stein's libretto.

xxviii.   Gertrude Stein First Reader and Three Plays (1948)

1. Sugrue, Thomas. "With No Stein Unturned." *New*

York Herald Tribune, 7 March 1948, Sec. 7, p. 2.

First Reader is the "ultimate book." "Children are apt to
think the book quite sensible. Adults will like its music."

"In these last fragments of her work Miss Stein is concerned
almost wholly with the joyful sound of Anglo-Saxon words,
with the rhythm of thought as it breaks and spills into
speech, with the lovely patterns of sound and idea which
cluster around the edge of awareness. The joy of the writer is
obvious in every matching pair of words, and it is a joy
which finds easy access to a reader's mind." (Cf. II-A-2.)

2. Bogan, Louise. "Great-Aunt Gertrude, Half-
   Asleep." *New York Times,* 28 March 1948, Sec. 7, p. 6.

   First Reader "is the combination of a marvelous ear with a
   lively sense of life's incongruously matched minutiae that
   gives the more 'conscious' Stein productions power, sparkle and
   interest. . . . Her stories are full of ancient metamorphoses,
   horrible surprises, shocks and terror, as well as gentler subjects
   and themes."

xxix.   Blood on the Dining Room Floor (1948)

1. Fremantle, Anne. "Whodunits, in a Variety of
   Keys." *New York Times,* 1 August 1948, Sec. 7, p. 13.

   Blood strikes a balance between *Three Lives* and *Brewsie and
   Willie.* "Tension and sleuthing in this story are as vivid and
   real as that rose was red."

xxx. Last Operas and Plays (1949)

1. Redman, Ben Ray. "Word-Intoxicated Woman."
   Saturday Review, (2 April 1949), 18-19.

   Last Operas and Plays is a book neither of operas nor of plays,
   save for *Yes Is for a Very Young Man* and *Four Saints in Three
   Acts.* Stein lacks discipline.

2. Rogers, W. G. "Gertrude Stein Hovering." *New York Herald Tribune,* 3 April 1949, Sec. 7, p. 6.

Vaguely about *Last Operas and Plays,* this article includes the following: "If her writing is full of repetitions, her writings in a large sense are not repetitious." ". . . how diversified her creative endowment was, how wide her interests, how for her the world was not one thing but uncountably many."

3. Farrelly, John. "Homespun Sibyl." *New Republic,* 120 (16 May 1949), 18-19.

"In this book, when she does deliver straight from the horse's mouth, the common sense strikes as commonplace, as trite as it is true." Farrelly implies that Stein withdrew from the public and became noncommunicative.

4. Bernstein, Leonard. "Music and Miss Stein." *New York Times,* 22 May 1949, Sec. 7, p. 4.

Bernstein's criticism drifts from Stein to Ernest Hemingway et al., to Virgil Thomson to Aaron Copland. On Stein: ". . . she was very funny." "It is a humor of destruction: a humor which, like that of the Marx Brothers, negates commonly accepted axioms of reality, and leaves the perceiver dangling, reeling, and grateful for the urge that enables him to agree with organized chaos by the simple act of laughing."

On Stein and music: "Stein has come closer than any other writer except Joyce to the medium of music." "She is able to musicalize words." Thomson's music will be as important in music history as Stein's texts in literary history.

5. Taubman, Howard. "Theater: Stein Revival." *New York Times,* 6 March 1963, p. 7.

Yes Is for a Very Young Man "does not work out in the theater"; "does not come alive as drama."

xxxi.   Things As They Are (1950)

1. Fitts, Dudley. "Q. E. D." *New York Times,* 24 December 1950, Sec. 7, p. 11.

Things As They Are "is young writing; but it is, on the whole,
surprisingly well controlled." "Tactile language" is
Stein's "greatest contribution to contemporary literature."

2. Wilson, Edmund. Review of *Things As They Are*. *New
   Yorker*, 27 (15 September 1951), 125-31. Reprinted
   in Edmund Wilson, *The Shores of Light: A Literary
   Chronicle of the Twenties and Thirties*. New York: Farrar,
   Straus, and Young, 1952.

   Things As They Are "is a product of some literary merit
   and of much psychological interest." Wilson thought earlier
   that the growing unintelligibility of Stein's work was "partly
   due to a need imposed by the problem of writing about
   relationships between women of a kind that the standards
   of that era would not have allowed her to describe more
   explicitly. . . ."

xxxii. Two: Gertrude Stein and Her Brother and Other Early Pieces (1908-1912) (1951)

1. Havighurst, Walter. "More for Gertrude Stein
   Devotees—and a Biografy." *Chicago Sunday Tribune*,
   23 September 1951, Sec. 4, p. 6.

2. Rogers, W.G. "Sound Keeps on Sounding." *Saturday
   Review*, 34 (29 September 1951), 16-17.
   Two is "intense, compact, and rewarding."

3. Frankenberg, Lloyd. "Gertrude Stein's Reality."
   New York Times, 30 September 1951, Sec. 7, p. 5.

4. Morris, Lloyd. "She Disconnected Quality from
   Subject." *New York Herald Tribune*, 28 October 1951,
   Sec. 6, p. 12.

5. Rudikoff, Sonya. "Clarity and Force in Gertrude Stein." *Hudson Review*, 5, No. 1 (Spring 1952), 148-54.

   Janet Flanner, in her introduction to *Two*, can only write about Stein through imitation of Stein.

6. Phelps, Robert. "Uses of Gertrude Stein." *Yale Review*, 45, No. 4 (June 1956), 600-03.

   Phelps, concerned with the first five volumes of Yale's *The Unpublished Writings of Gertrude Stein*, finds "the best skeleton key" to her work is *Composition As Explanation* (II-E-vi) and Wilder's introduction to *Four in America* (II-E-xxvi). Phelps criticizes Stein for not coming to terms with herself.

xxxiii.   Mrs. Reynolds and Five Earlier Novelettes (1931-1942) (1952)

1. Rosenfeld, Isaac. "Pleasures and Troubles." *New York Times*, 21 September 1952, Sec. 7, p. 6.

   Mrs. Reynolds is composed of a style combination of portrait and narrative devices. It is Stein's style "which first alienated the 'serious-minded', that is now winning for her the attention of the English Departments."

2. Anon. "Stein's Last Novel." *Time*, 60 (22 September 1952), 114 and 116.

   Although this article is mostly summary, the reviewer does say of *Mrs. Reynolds* that "it often reads like self-imitation, with its haphazard stenography of irrelevant chatter, its sleep-enticing rhythms, its delight in obsessive enumeration of uninteresting objects, and its aggravating tone of false naiveté."

3. Rogers, W.G. "Stein Stories, Lifelike in Their Way."
   New York Herald Tribune, 28 September 1952, Sec. 6,
   p. 7.

> *Mrs. Reynolds* contains "some obvious historical parallels."
> "There's history behind this, and underneath it. Miss Stein was
> writing, but on a different creative level, exactly what she
> was later to write and publish under the title 'Wars I
> Have Seen'."

4. Havighurst, Walter. "Words into Partitions." *Saturday
   Review*, 35 (4 October 1952), 35.

> *Mrs. Reynolds* "is a tantalizing and exasperating book,
> which can also be exhilarating in the measure that a reader
> likes to be thrown upon his own resources."

5. Sutherland, Donald. "A Lady of Letters." *New
   Republic*, 127 (6 October 1952), 26.

   See also II-E-xxxii-6.

xxxiv.   Bee Time Vine and Other Pieces (1913-1927) (1953)

1. Rogers, W.G. "And a Fact Is a Fact." *New York
   Times*, 8 November 1953, Sec. 7, p. 24.

> "Many of these pages have all of Miss Stein except the
> distinguishing, unforgettable edge, all of her except the very
> best. These seem to be exercises, or notebooks. . . . This
> near-accomplishment defines the real accomplishment more
> clearly than anything else could."

2. Anon. Review of *Bee Time Vine and Other Pieces*. *New
   Yorker*, 30 (6 March 1954), 119-20.

   See II-E-xxxii-6.

xxxv.   As Fine As Melanctha (1914-1930) (1954)

See II-E-xxxii-6.

xxxvi.   Painted Lace and Other Pieces (1914-1937) (1955)

1. Rogers, W.G. "Nothing, but Something." *New York Times*, 23 October 1955, Sec. 7, p. 12.

   "The pieces in this book were the splinter production of those thrilling years, the chips which fell as the major works , were hewn out."

   "As always when at her best, she uses double talk to arrive at plain meanings; she adds nothing and nothing and gets something; her sum is an emotional impact, an excitement, an undeniable deep stirring. This is the marvel and the mystery of her language; it can be an incantation, and like the lingo of the medicine man, it can say little while accomplishing a lot. . . ."

   See II-E-xxxii-6.

2. Millett, Fred B. Review of *Painted Lace and Other Pieces*. *American Literature*, 29 (May 1957), 222-23.

   The organization of the book might have been of more value if chronological. *Painted Lace* belongs to the "wastebasket school of literary scholarship," the adherents of which "believe that every verbal dribble, every verbal doodle of a writer of any reputation deserves scholarly publication." All in all, Millett cannot understand the publication of the so far five volumes of Stein's unpublished writings, and is evidently quite disturbed that these are being published rather than the "dozens of valuable scholarly manuscripts" which cannot be published for lack of funds.

xxxvii.   Stanzas in Meditation and Other Poems (1929-1933) (1956)

1. Fowlie, Wallace. "The State of Change." *Saturday Review*, 39 (22 December 1956), 20-21.

    Stanzas in Meditation "may be looked upon . . . as stylistic exercises which helped the writer to reach the extreme simplification in language for which she is famous." Her poetry comes from the relationship between her words and her thoughts. "A word used by Gertrude Stein does not designate a thing as much as it designates the way in which the thing is destroyed, or the way whereby the poet has learned to live with it."

2. Larkin, Philip. "You Do Something First." *Manchester Guardian*, 29 January 1957, p. 4.

    "Only the larger libraries need feel responsible about Miss Stein's poetry."

3. Anon. "Experiment in Destruction." *London Times Literary Supplement*, 56 (8 February 1957), 82.

    Stein's "aim was the total destruction of language." "She did at least discover perhaps half-a-dozen tricks of style that introduced new speech rhythms into prose; and, even if she did repeat each of the half-dozen perhaps ten thousand times, they were in the first place genuine discoveries." ". . . that this volume, and introduction [by Donald Sutherland], should be issued by a responsible University Press, is an astonishing monument to academic gullibility."

4. Shapiro, Karl. "Poetry in 1956." *Prairie Schooner*, 31 (Spring 1957), 11-16.

    A review of *Stanzas in Meditation* appears between pp. 15 and 16. Stein "is a great pedant. . . . She wrote as a poet would if a poet had never had a dream or a sleepless night. Somebody (Yale) is trying to make Gertrude out as a poet."
    On "I wish now to wish now": "The dismal unoriginality of this idea and the abysmal and conscious stupidity of the poem are exemplary of the whole book."

5. Ashbery, John. "The Impossible." *Poetry,* 90 (July
   1957), 250-54.

> *Stanzas in Meditation* will probably please readers who are
> satisfied only by literary extremes, but who have not
> previously taken to Miss Stein because of a kind of lack of
> seriousness in her work, characterized by lapses into
> dull, facile rhyme; by the over-employment of rhythms
> suggesting a child's incantation against grownups; and by
> monotony. There is certainly plenty of monotony in the
> 150-page title poem which forms the first half of this volume,
> but it is the fertile kind, which generates excitement as
> water monotonously flowing over a dam generates
> electrical power. The austere "stanzas" are made up almost
> entirely of colorless connecting words . . . though now
> and then Miss Stein throws in an orange, a lilac or an
> Albert to remind us that it really is the world, our world,
> that she has been talking about. The result is like certain
> monochrome [Willem] de Kooning paintings in which
> isolated strokes of color take on a deliciousness they
> never could have had out of context, or a piece of music
> by [Anton von] Webern in which a single note on the
> celesta suddenly irrigates a whole desert of dry, scratchy
> sounds in the strings.
> Ashbery goes on to examine "Stanzas in Meditation." He
> is reminded of *Golden Bowl* and *Sacred Fount,* "which
> seem to strain with a superhuman force toward 'the condition
> of music', of poetry." The other poems in *Stanzas* are charming,
> "though lacking the profundity of" "Stanzas."
> *"Stanzas in Meditation* is no doubt the most successful of
> her attempts to do what can't be done, to create a counterfeit
> of reality more real than reality. And if, on laying the
> book aside, we feel that it is still impossible to accomplish
> the impossible, we are also left with the conviction that it is
> the only thing worth trying to do."

6. Yalden-Thomson, D.C. "Obscurity, Exhibitionism,
   and Gertrude Stein." *Virginia Quarterly Review,* 34
   (Winter 1958), 133-37.

See II-C-128.

xxxviii.   Alphabets and Birthdays (1957)

1. Rogers, W.G. "Lovely Paper, Lovely Pens." *New York Times*, 24 November 1957, Sec. 7, p. 12.
    Stein is often imitated but inimitable.

2. Yalden-Thomson, D.C. See II-E-xxxvii-6.

    Yalden-Thomson divides Stein's writings into three categories: the early, and perhaps greatest, works; the idiosyncratic; the comprehensible. *Alphabets and Birthdays* contains some of each of the last two categories.

xxxix.   A Novel of Thank You (1958)

xl.   Selected Writings of Gertrude Stein (1946; 1962)

1. Lerman, Leo. "A Wonderchild for 72 Years." *Saturday Review*, 29 (2 November 1946), 17-18.

2. Miller, Perry. "Steinese." *New York Times*, 3 November 1946, Sec. 7, pp. 6 and 30.
    This review tends to be mostly a biographical synopsis strung together with quotations. Miller criticizes the bad proofreading job done on the book, and the "slight notes." "This sort of whimsy among her defenders has done more than ridicule among her detractors to obscure her real significance."

3. Anon. Review of *Selected Writings of Gertrude Stein*. *New Yorker*, 22 (9 November 1946), 124.

4. Cowley, Malcolm. "Gertrude Stein: Writer or Word Scientist?" *New York Herald Tribune*, 24 November 1946, Sec. 8, p. 1.
    Cowley asks why admiring critics or close friends have not attempted to explain what Stein meant to say. He feels "she will live more in her remembered personality than in her

works." "Her style is like a chemical useless in its pure state but powerful when added to other mixtures. American prose has changed its whole direction partly because of Gertrude Stein."

xli.   Gertrude Stein's America (1965)

xlii.   In Circles

1. Barnes, Clive. "Theater: Gertrude Stein Words at the Judson Church." *New York Times*, 14 October 1967, p. 12.

    Barnes refers to Stein as "the mother of us all" and to *In Circles* as a play "urgent with the newness of tomorrow." The article contains information on stage sets, director, composer, and so on. Barnes subtly wishes Stein would have more influence on American drama than Tennessee Williams, Arthur Miller, or the early Edward Albee.

2. Regelson, Rosalyn. "Was She Mother of Us All?" *New York Times*, 5 November 1967, Sec. 2, p. 1.

    In Circles is "a gnomic playlet printed in short sentences and paragraphs, the words and phrases charged with amazing vitality though they have no 'meaning'." Regelson writes a psychological critique of current American drama, and discusses *Mother of Us All* (II-E-xxvii) as "Miss Stein's last and greatest work," which had "expanding freedom" compared to current dramas.

3. Sullivan, Dan. "Another Delightful Look at 'In Circles', a Drama of Obfuscation." *New York Times*, 28 June 1968, p. 36.

    Sullivan comments on the stage directions.

xliii.   Look at Me Now and Here I Am (1968)

1. Anon. "Patient Monument." *London Times Literary Supplement*, 8 August 1968, p. 845.

    Stein "could be a first-class literary critic when she chose." "In general, a reading-aloud from this Gertrude Stein anthology may nowadays be found an easier exercise than an attempt to follow Miss Allegra Stewart [II-A-15]."

xliv.   Gertrude Stein on Picasso (1970)

1. Mellow, James R. *"Gertrude Stein on Picasso."* New *York Times*, 20 December 1970, Sec. 7, pp. 4 and 21.

    Gertrude Stein on Picasso is "a beautiful specimen of book making." ". . . the selection printed here . . . consists of half-formulated ideas and bare, misspelled working notes" (in reference to the scant notebook material included). The book contains "an illustrated catalogue of the Picasso works—with some unexplained omissions. . . ."

2. Kenner, Hugh. "The Seemingly Wise." *New Republic*, 164 (16 January 1971), 25-26 +.

    "If you buy the book you'll have bought a chunk of history, as mute and in its way as authentic as a fossil." Kenner refers to the "colorful litter" of Gertrude Stein Month, December 1970.

3. Anon. Review of *Gertrude Stein on Picasso*. *Choice*, 8 (June 1971), 541.

    Other Picasso books *"use* the Stein material"; this "essential art book" *"presents* it."

xlv. Fernhurst, Q.E.D., and Other Early Writings (1971)

1. Loercher, Diane. "Gertrude Stein in the Beginning."
   Christian Science Monitor, 7 October 1971, p. 6.
   "The collection, as placed in context by Mr. [Donald]
   Gallup, is also a superb initiation into the mysteries of
   Miss Stein." Loercher finds "irritating" the bibliographical
   information Gallup gives in "A Note on the Texts."
   "Each story smolders like an adolescent romance assuming
   a self-importance that seems undeserved."

2. Buckman, Peter. "Summer Uplift." *New Statesman*, 84
   (4 August 1972), 169.

xlvi. Primer for the Gradual Understanding
of Gertrude Stein (1971)

xlvii. Volume I of the Previously Uncollected Writings
of Gertrude Stein: Reflection on the Atomic
Bomb (1973)

See II-D-26 and II-E-xlviii.

xlviii. Volume II of the Previously Uncollected
Writings of Gertrude Stein: How Writing Is
Written (1974)

See II-D-27.

1. Zinnes, Harriet. "Lively Syndicate of Modernism."
   Nation, 218 (18 May 1974), 631-32 and 634.

   Atomic Bomb is, after the *Primer*, "a good place to begin to
   get a quick feeling for Stein." Zinnes makes some interesting
   remarks on Stein's "pleasantness."

2. Sutherland, Donald. "The Pleasures of Gertrude
   Stein." *New York Review of Books*, 21 (30 May 1974),
   28-30.

   Sutherland finds "depressing and diminishing" the freedom
   [?] to "interpret a great deal of Gertrude Stein's work as more
   or less camouflaged accounts of lesbianism." Robert Bartlett
   Haas (II-D-26) "should write a whole book"; he "is both
   familiar with her work and sympathetic with her more extreme
   experiments." Sutherland criticizes Haas for being sometimes
   "cryptic and scrappy" in his "little introductions."

3. Beer, Patricia. "At the Court of Queen Gertrude."
   London Times Literary Supplement, 8 November 1974,
   p. 1252.

   It is more important to be T. S. Eliot or James Joyce than
   Gertrude Stein.

F. Reviews of Secondary Literature

i. W.G. Rogers. *When This You See Remember Me* (I-B-i-11)

1. Bennett, Peggy. "Doughboy and a Shepherdess." *Saturday Review*, 31 (10 July 1948), 17.

   The worst parts of the book are Rogers's attempts to defend Stein. *When This You See* is "droll"; Bennett does not really criticize Stein.

2. Thomson, Virgil. "Gertrude Stein Portrayed by an Old Friend." *New York Herald Tribune*, 11 July 1948, Sec. 7, p. 3.

   Rogers's is the "fullest speaking portrait of Miss Stein that has yet appeared and the only one of Miss Toklas with which this reader is acquainted." Rogers sees Stein's life "as a continuum, the constant spectacle of a mind at work."

3. Thompson, Ralph. "Gertrude Stein, As a Visiting American Recalls Her." *New York Times*, 1 August 1948, Sec. 7, p. 6.

   This is a synopsis of *When This You See*. Rogers "may be accused of underrating Miss Stein's disingenuousness in some respects, but hardly, under the circumstances, of overrating her charm. His amiable recollections, the letters he reprints and his unpretentious critical comments, make his memoir the best yet of its kind for the general reader."

4. Watts, Richard, Jr. "Woman into Myth." *New Republic*, 119 (9 August 1948), 24-25.

   Rogers's is a "warm, brightly informal account." "To one who remains among the skeptics, though, his portrait is but added proof that Gertrude Stein was distinguished and important, not as a writer, but as a great personality and influence, usually for good, on other writers."

   Included is the following unexplained remark: "Her political orientation remains a dark spot on the reputation of one of the most notable literary figures of the first half of the twentieth century."

5. Anon. "Makers of Wonder Bread." *Time*, 52 (16 August 1948), 96, 98 and 100.

> The only really interesting thing about this short synopsis is the consistent reference of the reviewer to Miss Toklas's nickname "Pussy." Rogers mentions both Alice's and Gertrude's nicknames in his biography, and one wonders if either gentleman were totally aware of the implications.

6. Stull, Carolyn. "A GI and a Very Fine Lady: Gertrude Stein." *San Francisco Chronicle: This World*, 29 August 1948, pp. 18 and 20.

> This review has some dates wrong (i.e., *Everybody's Autobiography* published in 1932). Rogers's book is a "description of his friendship with her and of Miss Stein herself as he knew her."

ii. **Donald Sutherland**. *Gertrude Stein: A Biography of Her Work* (II-A-16)

1. Walter Havighurst.

> Sutherland's is an "informal and illuminating discussion." See II-E-xxxii-1.

2. W.G. Rogers.

> Sutherland "interprets the novels most helpfully, in particular the romantic 'Lucy Church Amiably' and the existential 'Ida'," although his work suffers sometimes from foggy elucidation. See II-E-xxxii-2.

3. Lloyd Frankenberg.

> *Gertrude Stein* "is a model of interpretive writing, clear, charming, witty, and with all the vitality that his use of the word 'biography' might lead us to expect." Sutherland is able to translate the notions of consciousness in the late nineteenth and early twentieth century into "thinkable" entities. See II-E-xxxii-3.

4. Lloyd Morris. See II-E-xxxii-4.

5. Sonya Rudikoff.

Sutherland's book is praised for its "unwavering critical focus" and its "use of various disciplines to illuminate [Stein's] work." On the other hand, he accepts too completely "her sensibility" (without dealing "with her personality") and ends up writing "his book as Miss Stein might have written it." "His formulation of critical problems employs her mannerisms, and his prose resembles that of her lectures. Questions are raised in her way, and it is her answers that are given, her terms that are used. . . ."

"At no point does [Sutherland] call into question the goals Miss Stein set for herself. He is indifferent to the themes or directions of her work which she does not state explicitly. His interest in her use of language does not go beyond her specific interest in language. He speaks of her intense devotion to the intellect, but it is invariably her own view of the intellect that directs him." See II-E-xxxii-5.

6. Anon. "No Question and No Answer." *London Times Literary Supplement*, 51 (4 April 1952), 236.

Sutherland's "is a work of sound scholarship and of engaging hero-worship, rather than of detached and balanced criticism." Despite that, it "has great charm. His syntax has a pleasant, slightly jolting roughness, and his manner a conversational directness, rare in academic literature, and owing something, but not slavishly, to the example of Miss Stein herself. He starts up ideas on every page, if he does not always run them down, and he has a pleasant if sometimes rash schoolboy taste for making phrases. . . . For a sober and definitive critical study of Miss Stein we shall have to wait for the work of an older and perhaps duller man. . . ."

7. Thomson, Virgil. "A Very Difficult Author." *New York Review of Books*, 16 (8 April 1971), 3-8.

Sutherland's is one of the three significant books for understanding Stein.

All subsequent critical works refer to Sutherland's study.

iii. Donald Gallup, ed. *Flowers of Friendship* (I-B-i-5)

1. Cowley, Malcolm. "Miss Stein Is Miss Stein." *New York Times*, 16 August 1953, Sec. 7, pp. 7 and 13.

   Gallup's "editorial work was done with unobtrusive tact, and the book, besides being easy to read, casts a somewhat new light on Miss Stein and her place in history." Cowley objects to the title because most of the letters were not from friends but from lessers (those who wanted something from Stein). The article contains a printer's error (?): 1953 is given as the date of publication for *Autobiography* instead of 1933. Cowley does not think the letters tell Stein's story, which must "be read by indirection."

   ". . . her talent was scientific or speculative instead of literary. Lacking from her equipment as a writer were the passion to communicate, the willingness to review and (although she was an engaging raconteur) the ability to construct a story. She was able, however, to turn her disabilities into advantages and to make experiments in language that other writers could use to the greatest advantage."

   "She left behind her the memory of a personage—not a great writer but a bold experimenter and a great woman."

2. Scott, Winfield Townley. "When Miss Stein Held Literary Court and the Postman Seldom Rested." *New York Herald Tribune*, 16 August 1953, Sec. 6, pp. 1 and 6.

   Scott thinks that Gallup did a good job of editing *Flowers of Friendship* but asks if the book was necessary. "What we have here are the materials for biography, but not *used*, merely presented, and inevitably surrounded by a heap of trivia which is of no biographical value." Scott objects to Stein being only "faintly echoed—faintly mirrored" in the book. There is much around about the "Old Lady," some about her career, but much more material that belongs in biographies of the other figures—Ernest Hemingway, F. Scott Fitzgerald, Ford Madox Ford.

3. Geismar, Maxwell. "A Friend Is Stein." *Saturday Review*, 36 (22 August 1953), 19-20.

The *Flowers of Friendship* is seen as an expression of the same admiration and uncertainty Geismar feels toward Stein. Some letters, which seem to carry "the truth about a human being" "are worth pages of official literary criticism." The book offers a "panorama of the whole period," not a clarification of Stein and/or of her work.

4. Wagenknecht, Edward. "Those Letters to Gertrude Stein: 'Isn't Writing a Hard Job Though?' " *Chicago Sunday Tribune*, 23 August 1953, Sec. 4, p. 6.

In reviewing *Flowers of Friendship*, Wagenknecht remarks, "since these are all letters TO Gertrude Stein, it is quite possible to read them."

5. Cannell, Kathleen. "She Liked to See Them Come and Go." *Christian Science Monitor*, 3 September 1953, p. 11.

Cannell praises Gallup's editing of *Flowers of Friendship* for, "in selecting letters from the 20,000 bequested by Gertrude Stein to the Yale University Library, in placing them in 'chapters' according to their period, and in composing brief links to illuminate personalities and situations, Curator Donald Gallup has proved a remarkably clear-sighted and sensitive editor. . . . He has produced a highly entertaining book, more exciting and authentic than most personal biographies."

6. Saroyan, William. "Some Thoughts about Gertrude Stein." *Reporter*, 9 (13 October 1953), 39-40.

Mr. Gallup chose well the letters and editions of letters printed in *Flowers of Friendship*. The letters reveal Stein as a person through the eyes of her acquaintances—although many parts of the story are left hanging. Stein "was a writer's writer."

7. Stallman, Robert Wooster. "The Flowers of
   Friendship." *Sewanee Review*, 64 (Spring 1955), 317-23.
   "They are friendly letters on the whole, but they are not
   in the main letters that flowered from friendship." Stallman
   writes that "the manuscript of *The Making of Americans*
   circulated among publishers for almost two decades. . . ."
   There are printer's errors in the article. Stallman feels Gallup
   "under-edited" the book.

iv. Elizabeth Sprigge. *Gertrude Stein* (I-B-i-16)

1. Hamilton, Iain. "Funny Being a Genius." *Spectator*,
   198 (25 January 1957), 117.
   Hamilton takes a very dim view of Stein, who had a feeling
   for the visual but erred in attempting to transfer it into words.

2. Philip Larkin. See II-E-xxxvii-2.
   "Miss Sprigge leaves her readers anxious to judge
   for themselves [re Stein's literary worth], which is
   one of the surest signs that her book is a success."

3. Anon. See II-E-xxxvii-3.
   "Miss Sprigge is herself more than half-deluded by her
   [Stein], but her biography is full and accurate and pleasantly
   written. . . ."

4. Russell, Francis. "Stein Biography." *Christian Science
   Monitor*, 21 February 1957, p. 7.
   "Elizabeth Sprigge's biography is an interesting and
   sprightly book." Russell treats Stein seriously at the very least
   because "she has been taken seriously" and because of "the
   brickbats she has tossed at established English usage." He
   thinks time is on the side of those who believe that "that which
   does not make sense is senseless as well as pointless."

5. Rolo, Charles J. "Reader's Choice." *Atlantic Monthly*,
   199 (March 1957), 80.

   Sprigge's *Gertrude Stein* "is admirably documented, ably
   written, and continuously interesting."

6. Guthrie, Ramon. "Gertrude Stein's Many-Sided
   Personality: She Was Where Paris Was Where the
   Century Was." *New York Herald Tribune Book Review*,
   33 (3 March 1957), 4.

7. Anon. Review of Elizabeth Sprigge's *Gertrude Stein*.
   New Yorker, 33 (16 March 1957), 150.

   Sprigge's book is mentioned as "only a trifle more objective
   and, inevitably, quite a bit less entertaining" than *The
   Autobiography of Alice B. Toklas*, although Sprigge's is "possibly
   more factually accurate."

8. Harrison, Gilbert A. "Gertrude Stein and the
   Nay-Sayers." *New Republic*, 136 (18 March 1957),
   17-18.

   Sprigge's *Gertrude Stein* "does tell us many things we hadn't
   known before, her writing is pleasant and her reporting (not
   judgment, she gives us no judgment) is not unintelligent.
   Having said that I can think of nothing more worth saying
   about her book." Harrison deals with the reception of this book,
   and with critics' negative judgment of Stein. Neither Sprigge
   nor the critics, however, answer the question "Why was
   Gertrude Stein so influential?" Harrison's answer: "It was
   because there was a ruthless rightness about her judgments
   concerning creativity. She was exceptionally alert, she did not
   talk or write to please others, what she knew she *knew*. . . .
   [Her] simplicity was the result of intense concentration. She
   meditated about how we know whatever we know, she
   thought about time and how all that changes from generation
   to generation and from place to place is the externals and our
   way of looking at them. She used words as if they were alive,
   exploring them singly and in relation to each other, regarding
   them as if they had been born this instant. She had no use for
   hand-me-downs: the present was her preoccupation. The force
   of her vision knocked pretensions flat. . . ."

9. Spender, Stephen. "Three Lives Make One." *New York Times*, 24 March 1957, Sec. 7, p. 3.

   This is not so much a review of *Gertrude Stein* as it is a rehashing of Stein's life and work. "Perhaps the style for which she was famous was a formula arrived at as a compromise between innate deficiencies and remarkable insights."

10. Redman, Ben Ray. "Priestess of the Lost Generation." *Saturday Review*, 40 (20 April 1957), 16-17.

    Sprigge's biography has many quotations, draws on critics and *Autobiography of Alice B. Toklas*, and contains little personal criticism of Stein. "The narrative is well organized, the style is pleasing, and the author modestly refrains from coming between her subject and her readers."

11. Mayne, Richard. "The Great Stone Face." *New Statesman and Nation*, 53 (27 April 1957), 550.

    Gertrude Stein "has the virtues and limitations of objectivity: she [Sprigge] knows all about Gertrude Stein, but seems fundamentally uninvolved."

12. Morgan, Edwin. Review of *Gertrude Stein*. *America*, 97 (27 April 1957), 138-39.

    Sprigge's biography is an "excellent portrait of Miss Stein."

13. Sutherland, Donald. "Gertrude Stein." *Nation*, 184 (27 April 1957), 373-74.

    Sprigge's biography contains some inaccuracies. "One might want a more continuous imagination of the inward scale and force of the life lived, and less circumstantial chatter. . . ."

14. D.C. Yalden-Thomson. See II-E-xxxvii-6.

    Sprigge's biography is an excellent and sympathetic study. There are, according to Yalden-Thomson, three omissions. "Elizabeth Sprigge has nothing to say about the more intimate aspects of her life." "While her capacity for friendship is explained, her capacity to quarrel is not." Sprigge omits any "study of the aims of her curious compositions."

15. Hilary Corke. See II-C-128.

16. Virgil Thomson. See II-F-ii-7.

v.   Benjamin Reid. *Art by Subtraction* (II-A-12)

1. Frankenberg, Lloyd. "Her Place on the Shelf." *New York Times*, 15 June 1958, Sec. 7, p. 4.

   Art by Subtraction "is the first full-scale, closely reasoned, documented attempt to downgrade Gertrude Stein. . . ." Reid's book begins well, with some enthusiasm, but slowly dwindles to the dispassionate, to the guarded, and finally, on p. 85, to the tirade. Frankenberg, despite his obvious bias, attempts to deal objectively with the "dissenting opinion." The theoretical discussions in the early part of the book are due to the fact that "the author is at home in theory."

   See Samuel Hubert McMillan, Jr.'s, dissertation (II-B-17).

vi.   John Malcolm Brinnin. *Third Rose* (I-B-i-2)

1. Maddocks, Melvin. " 'So Daring . . . So Foolish'." *Christian Science Monitor*, 12 November 1959, p. 15.

   Brinnin's is "an admirably clear account of Miss Stein's slow flowering into her own kind of literary cubism." "Shooting up, surrounding, and at times almost choking the third rose is a vast proliferation of miscellaneous fact, anecdote, and high literary gossip."

2. Shattuck, Roger. "Mother of Them All." *Saturday Review*, 42 (14 November 1959), 28.

   Brinnin's *Third Rose* has a few minor errors and omissions in a vast amount of information and interpretation. Brinnin "probes far beyond earlier biographies into the deep-seated contradictions which beset an artist's life."

3. Anon. "Abominable Snowoman." *Time*, 74 (16 November 1959), 126-28.

> *Time* approaches *Third Rose* as a "biographically complete if critically indulgent account of the concentric odyssey of Gertrude Stein," who "tried to purify words by divorcing them from meanings and using them as pigments or notes." The result, claims this reviewer, "was a kind of singing non-commercial." "Concentric odyssey" per *Time* is: in her beginning was her end, because she was all middle.

4. Frankenberg, Lloyd. "Simply Confoundingly New." *New York Times*, 6 December 1959, Sec. 7, p. 4.

> *The Third Rose* is well balanced in the choice and number of quotations. Frankenberg suggests that it is an entertaining biography. " 'The Third Rose' provides much of the narrative thread, the specific features, that Gertrude Stein by intention omitted, without doing violence to that intention; and without disturbing the separate roses, the book gathers them into a handsome, wittily gallant bouquet."

5. Scott, Winfield Townley. "Gertrude Stein's Extraordinary Personality and Experimental Prose." *New York Herald Tribune Book Review*, 36, No. 20 (20 December 1959), 3.

> Brinnin's *Third Rose* is a well-written book of biography and criticism.

6. Holzhauer, Jean. "A Journey through the World of Gertrude Stein." *Commonweal*, 71 (22 January 1960), 473.

> Brinnin has done an "impressive quantity of research." His prose is obscure, cute. "It is useful to have all this reminiscence in a single volume, and it is not Mr. Brinnin's fault that his story is so well foreknown, even to the death scene. . . ." There is no "sense of actual confrontation" in *Third Rose*.

7. Anon. "Briefly Noted." *New Yorker*, 35 (30 January 1960), 107.

> This very brief review states that "An unflinching discretion smothers every page, and if there is nothing inflammatory,

there is also nothing original, or even resourceful, in the
matter of either information or insight."

8. McLuhan, Marshall. Review of *The Third Rose*.
   Canadian Forum, 39 (February 1960), 262.

9. Kazin, Alfred. "The Mystery of Gertrude Stein."
   Reporter, 22 (18 February 1960), 48 and 51-52.
   Reprinted in Alfred Kazin, *Contemporaries*. Boston:
   Little, Brown, 1962.

   Kazin does not find that Brinnin deals with the
   comprehensibility or existence of Stein's works. "My objection
   to his book is not that he overrates her work but that I cannot
   see a motivating reason for his own book. To write about
   Gertude Stein without justifying her work is, at this stage,
   simply to recall her fashionable doings. Mr. Brinnin manages
   not only to say all the right things about her work but to hold it
   at a distance, to make us feel that the work is not pressing,
   of secondary importance." Kazin feels Stein's work is "a
   curiosity, even a monstrosity, and has no part in our living
   and thinking."

10. Anon. "Reader's Guide." *Yale Review*, 49 (March
    1960), VI.

    "It is as biography that [Brinnin's] book is most successful."
    As criticism it is inadequate, save as criticism of writings up
    through *Tender Buttons*. Brinnin gives no real impressions of
    Stein's world between 1920 and 1940.
    "Mr. Brinnin makes some errors. His time sequences are not
    always strictly right . . . and some of the details are incorrect.
    His memory of Picasso's 'Young Girl with a Basket of
    Flowers' has played him false when he refers to it as a 'little'
    canvas. Olga Picasso was not the mother of Picasso's
    daughter Maia. Francis Rose did not come to Paris to see his
    first show after the Second World War. The editors of the
    Yale Poetry Review (not *Journal*) did not approach Miss Stein for
    her thoughts on the atomic bomb. Some of the artists' names
    are misspelled (Vallotton, Lipchipz, Riba-Revira)." At the same
    time, it is the "best single book treating both Miss Stein and
    her work," "a generally sympathetic portrait . . . which does
    make available a great deal of information."

11. Baro, Gene. "The Practice of Literature." *Nation*, 190 (9 April 1960), 320-21.

>   "One wishes that Mr. Brinnin's study, valuable as it is, had gone somewhat deeper into the exceptional factors of personality that allowed Miss Stein to function in the contexts that she did. . . . The bland discretion of these pages seems something of a fault. . . ."
>
>   Baro's article tends to be more of a discussion of the social and historical milieu in which Stein lived and of her existence as an artist, than a review of *Third Rose*.

12. Bradbury, Malcolm. "The American in Paris." *Manchester Guardian*, 20 May 1960, p. 9.

>   Bradbury's main complaint concerns documentation: no footnotes, no "precise acknowledgment of his sources," and no consistent effort to "establish dates."

13. Coleman, John. "Gertrude Stein Is a Nice Story." *Spectator*, 204 (20 May 1960), 739.

>   Primarily a review of *Third Rose*, Coleman's article also contains short comments on *Three Lives, Making of Americans* and *Tender Buttons*.

14. Pritchett, V. S. "The Old Covered Wagon." *New Statesman*, 59 (28 May 1960), 795-96.

>   *The Third Rose* "goes on too long" and "gets bogged down." Pritchett's review is partially a synopsis of Stein's character and personality. "All [James Joyce, Wyndham Lewis, Stein], except Gertrude Stein, made something of experiment. Hers failed. It was an intellectual failure."

15. Anon. "Stein's Way." *London Times Literary Supplement*, 59 (10 June 1960), 367.

>   Stein's "art is one of time-lag and after-effect."

16. Koch, Vivienne. "Three Lives." *Poetry*, 98 (April 1961), 59-62.

>   Koch includes a short review of *The Third Rose*. She classifies all but the very early work as poetry because, she writes, Stein

made "remote(r) translations from life." "Incantation" was the aim and method of Stein, William Butler Yeats, and Vachel Lindsay. There is a lack of proportion and humor in the analysis of Stein's attempts, although Brinnin does justice to her work. Stein's influence "lies chiefly in the reality as well as in the legend of her extraordinary personality."

17. Blöcker, Günter. "John Malcolm Brinnin: *Die Dritte Rose.*" *Literatur als Teilhabe: Kritische Orientierungen zur literarischen Gegenwart.* Berlin: Argon Verlag, 1966. Pp. 241-45.

This is mostly a discussion of Stein's works, her sense of words, her style.

18. Virgil Thomson. See II-F-ii-7.

Brinnin's is one of the three significant books for understanding Stein.

vii.   **Alice B. Toklas.** *What Is Remembered* (I-B-i-20)

1. Anon. Review of *What Is Remembered. Time,* 81 (22 March 1963), 97-98.

The reviewer sees this book by Toklas reading as though it were written by Stein; Toklas disappears "virtually without a trace into Gertrude Stein's life." "*What Is Remembered* is the sad, slight book of a woman who all her life has looked into a mirror and seen somebody else."

2. Barry, Joseph. "Miss Toklas on Her Own." *New Republic,* 148 (30 March 1963), 21-23.

Barry's review of *What Is Remembered* tends toward summary. Mr. Barry does devote the first page to Toklas, in a well-deserved effort to "rectify the error or at least to rescue the concept of *companion* and return it some of its ancient richness," and includes a few anecdotes to fill in the gap between Stein's death and the publication of this memoir.

3. Campbell, Colin. "Toklas Memoir." *Christian Science Monitor*, 4 April 1963, p. 17.

"What [Toklas] remembers ranges from delightful bagatelles to cultural profundities, all of it couched in a prose which has a way of husking an event to its core." "In addition to deft portraiture, rapier wit, and quintessential prose, 'What Is Remembered' offers insights of great power."

4. LeSage, Laurent. "Alice Speaks for Herself." *Saturday Review*, 46 (13 April 1963), 27.

What Is Remembered is "artlessly droll." It is Toklas here "whose handling of comic phrasing, timing, the terse statement, and the build-up that lets you down is so good it may be art or natural expression."

5. Baro, Gene. "A Memory Is a Memory Is a Memory." *New York Times*, 14 April 1963, Sec. 7, p. 44.

Alice Toklas "has her own way with words, a simplicity and reticence that is not artless, but that suggests meanings between and behind the lines."

6. Pryce-Jones, Alan. "Miss Toklas, This Time on Her Own." *New York Herald Tribune*, 21 April 1963, Sec. 6, p. 6.

What Is Remembered is "at times icily refreshing." Toklas "writes . . . a prose which seems natural to those who moved in the Stein world. . . . Sometimes this leads to a charming demureness." "But mostly the record is thin and cold. . . . It is also extremely inaccurate. On one illustration alone four out of eight people are mis-named, and the text has not been checked for slips." (There is, indeed, "one illustration alone" with eight people in it. See Ellen Wilson [I-B-23] for unforgivable errors.)

7. Holzhauer, Jean. "Thinking Back." *Commonweal*, 78 (10 May 1963), 206-07.

Holzhauer sees Toklas's style as an echo of Stein's. "Like Miss Stein, Miss Toklas depends more on the effects of an original personality—on style and tone—than on content."

8. Mellers, Wilfrid. "Autobiographies." *New Statesman*,
   66 (29 November 1963), 792.

> This review is more concerned with the *Autobiography of Alice
> B. Toklas* and *Three Lives* than with the autobiography of Alice
> B. Toklas. Mellers thinks that Stein's style influenced
> Toklas's. The *Autobiography* and *What Is Remembered* "are
> remarkably alike, yet distinct. They recount the same incidents,
> tell the same stories. Oddly enough, however, the version
> of Miss Toklas, to whom the events happened, seems neutral,
> numb, even denatured, compared with Gertrude Stein's
> vitality and gaiety."

9. Anon. "Emerging from Shadows." *London Times
   Literary Supplement*, 5 December 1963, p. 1007.

> In summarizing Toklas's memoirs, the reviewer mentions
> her "graceful slyness in manipulating her contacts and her
> prose." "Where it risks achieving permanence is . . . as a
> fragile work of art in its own right."

viii.   **Allegra Stewart.** *Gertrude Stein and the Present* (II-A-15)

1. Davis, Robert Gorham. "A Word Is a Word Is a
   Word." *New York Times*, 3 September 1967, Sec. 7,
   p. 5.

> Davis criticizes Stewart for some overly close, Jungian
> reading of Stein's works, although she has "put Gertrude
> Stein's whole creativity in much clearer light, by defining so
> fully its philosophical and psychological bases."

2. Wasserstrom, William. "*Gertrude Stein and the Present.*"
   American Literature, 40 (May 1968), 251-52.

> Stewart's is "the most persuasive case yet offered in support
> of Miss Stein's genius." Hers "is the first study of Gertrude
> Stein's imagination which performs feats of clarity undreamt
> of even by her admirers who long ago recognized in her
> language a sensible though mysterious principle of composition

to which she alone held the key." "What Miss Stewart demonstrates is that Gertrude Stein's psychology and metaphysics are incontrovertibly Jungian, that her language is marked not by a disregard of meaning but by solicitude of the most exacting kind, a passion for the root meaning of words. . . ."

3. Anon. See II-E-xliii-1.

Stewart's book is helpful only when read with Stein's books.

4. Virgil Thomson. See II-F-ii-7.

ix.   **Richard Bridgman.** *Gertrude Stein in Pieces*
      (II-A-2)

1. Kenner, Hugh. "Legend of the Rue de Fleurus." *National Review*, 23 (26 January 1971), 89-90.

2. Howard, Richard. "Literary Inventory." *New York Times*, 21 February 1971, Sec. 7, Part 1, pp. 5 and 26.

Howard reads Stein "less and less" because of the "mythologists, chief among them Gertrude Stein. If it were not for periodic reminders . . . I believe we should be circulating no more than the same images, the same stories, the same quotations. . . . Remarks are what we have come to expect of her, citations what we look for. . . ."
Bridgman's study "makes available the legacy of a mind he aptly labels forbidding in bulk and perplexing in manner, and in so doing he accounts for the likelihood of our neglect."

3. Virgil Thomson. See II-F-ii-7.

Bridgman's is one of the three significant books for understanding Stein. Thomson goes to great lengths to correct some of Bridgman's errors.

4. Anon. *"Gertrude Stein in Pieces* by Richard Bridgman."
   New Republic, 164 (10 April 1971), 28.

   Bridgman's is "by far the most intelligent analysis of Miss
   Stein's development as a writer that we have had. It is a
   splendid piece of scholarship—lucid, comprehensive, plausible"
   and Stein is a "writer's teacher more than the public's author."

5. Hoffman, Michael J. Review of *Gertrude Stein in Pieces,*
   By Richard Bridgman. *American Literature,* 43
   (November 1971), 467-68.

   Bridgman's is the culminating work of "two decades that
   have seen more than a half a dozen books" on Stein. His
   "scholarship is impeccable." However, because he "is so
   concerned with the ways Stein's writings reflect her inner
   turmoil . . . he minimizes the fun in her work and treats her too
   solemnly. . . . Someone finally had to do what Mr. Bridgman has
   done, and take a look at everything. Still, in reading his book
   one hungers for what is now possible: to examine Stein as a
   leading exemplar of literary modernism and try to speculate
   from her work about what was really going on in the
   breakthrough into modern art."
   Bridgman's is "a standard work in the field." Brinnin's
   speculations, however, are more interesting in regard to the
   work that must now be done on Stein.

6. Fendelman, Earl. "Happy Birthday, Gertrude Stein."
   American Quarterly, 27 (March 1975), 99-107.

   Bridgman is criticized for not noting the ignoring of "Stein's
   aesthetic principles." Stein is isolated in his work—he provides no
   real milieu. On the other hand, Bridgman provides "a
   greater historical precision than has ever before been brought
   to bear on Stein's career."
   Fendelman's article is concise, informative, and critical. He
   asks good questions and provides ideas for future studies.

x. **Irene Gordon, ed.** *Four Americans in Paris* (II-A-5)

1. Virgil Thomson. See II-F-ii-7.

2. Earl Fendelman. See II-F-ix-6.

xi. **Norman Weinstein.** *Gertrude Stein and the Literature of the Modern Consciousness* (II-A-17)

1. Earl Fendelman. See II-F-ix-6.

xii. **Alice B. Toklas.** *Staying on Alone* (I-B-i-21)

1. Grumbach, Doris. "Fine Print." *New Republic*, 169 (8 December 1973), 30 and 32.

    This unimportant review contains biographical errors.

2. Leibowitz, Herbert. "Queen Gertrude, Her Lady-in-Waiting and Her Court." *New York Times*, 3 February 1974, Sec. 7, pp. 1-2.

    Leibowitz never really deals with Toklas's letters, "a splendid collection" which "reveals [Toklas] as a remarkable woman in her own right. . . ."

3. Haynes, Muriel. "After Gertrude." *Ms.*, 2 (March 1974), 32 and 36.

4. Wyndham, Francis. "H. de Dactyl." *New Statesman*, 87 (1 March 1974), 298-300.

    The chronology in this review is confused and confusing. The letters are "gallant, honest, articulate and extremely amusing."

5. Levy, Paul. "Catering for Old Stoneface." *Observer Review*, 7 April 1974, p. 37.

    Alice B. Toklas, "prettier and wittier than Gertrude Stein," was "surely the better writer." The "very full index" of *Staying on Alone* "is inaccurate."

6. Thomson, Virgil. "Wickedly Wonderful Widow." *New York Review of Books*, 21 (7 March 1974), 12-15.

For some strange reason, Thomson refers to a "French friend convicted of wartime collaboration" but does not mention the name; he also omits the name from a quoted letter. Anyone at all familiar with Stein knows the reference is to Bernard Faÿ; why, then, the omission?

Thomson corrects some of the "unimportant errata"; he criticizes the book for its index, for the selection of letters, its "style," and "negligence about checking dates, proper names, and foreign language references."

Besides being a review and criticism of *Staying on Alone*, this is an interesting article on Toklas.

7. Dick, Kay. "Alice in Lonelyland." *Spectator*, 323 (13 April 1974), 453-54.

This review begins with a long, sarcastic one-paragraph review of *Autobiography*. Dick calls Alice's "a shadow role" and criticizes Stein's will, in which very little goes to Alice. She also completely ridicules the relationship between Gertrude and Alice, with Stein playing the role of baby and Toklas of mother (based on the Woojums' nicknames).

"In themselves they [the letters] are not greatly impressive" although "much material here will be of peripheral use to future biographers and literary historians." "The overall impression of Alice is one of evasion, or rather of a person so suppressed during Gertrude's lifetime that emancipation as an individual in her own right seems a losing battle."

8. Rudikoff, Sonya. "The Mama of Dada." *Commentary*, 57 (May 1974), 80-82 and 84-86.

9. Harriet Zinnes. See II-E-xlviii-1.

10. Patricia Beer. See II-E-xlviii-3.

Burns should have inserted "omission marks. He deletes freely but does not show us where. He is also rather erratic with his footnotes."

11. Earl Fendelman. See II-F-ix-6.

12. Flanner, Janet. "Memory Is All." *New Yorker*, 51 (15 December 1975), pp. 141-42, 144, 147-48, 150, 153-54.

   Flanner's article is a remembrance; among other things, she attempts to summarize Toklas's book.

xiii.   James Mellow. *Charmed Circle* (I-B-i-9)

1. Broyard, Anatole. "Monolithic Miss Stein." *New York Times*, 30 January 1974, p. 33.

   Broyard thinks Alice Toklas the "heroine" of *Charmed Circle*, which is a good book. Stein's "two greatest successes" can be explained: *Autobiography* is in Toklas's voice, and *Four Saints in Three Acts* had Virgil Thomson and Frederick Ashton to make it a success.

   Broyard is very obviously anti-Stein; among other things, Stein was known because of the celebrities around her, and Ernest Hemingway would have been better off without her advice.

   Mellow's biography is without the strong positive-negative reaction which Stein usually draws forth.

2. Harrison, Gilbert A. "Gertrude Stein and Company." *New Republic*, 170 (2 February 1974), 22-23.

   Charmed Circle is "an absorbing account." "Mr. Mellow's book is factual but entertaining, and by comparison with its two predecessors (biographies by John Malcolm Brinnin and Sylvia Spriggie [sic]) comprehensive."

   Harrison disagrees with some of Mellow's "facts"—valid disagreements concerning the myth and/or supposedly unsupported facts—which, however, are mentioned in other books. Among the items disagreed with are Alice's chain-smoking "all her life" and her rejoining the Catholic Church.

3. Herbert Leibowitz. See II-F-xii-2.

   Charmed Circle "consolidates rather than extends our understanding of an extraordinary time and its heroic actors.

[Mellow's] book lacks the intellectual excitement of discovery
that made Richard Bridgman's 'Gertrude Stein in Pieces'
so valuable." Mellow does not allow literary criticism to
intrude.

4. Young, Mahouri Sharp. "Life with Gertrude." *Art
   News*, 73 (April 1974), 92.

    This is a very illiterate review/criticism of Stein. See also
    p. 93 for a review of the Cone Collection.

5. Paul Levy. See II-F-xii-5.

    Mellow's biography "is more lucidly written than anything
    by its subject," who is referred to as "the first American
    expatriate with a crew-cut."

6. Sonya Rudikoff. See II-F-xii-8.

    Mellow is very good on the 1920s and adequate on the
    late 1930s and World War II. "He had wanted to write about
    Gertrude Stein the real person, not the legend, and he has
    succeeded." Stein and Alice B. Toklas were "Jamesian
    heroine[s]." Rudikoff writes some on Stein's "work," but her
    conclusions are unclear.

7. Harriet Zinnes. See II-E-xlviii-1.

    The weak point in Mellow's book is that "he is less keen on
    depicting the nuances of the work of Stein. . . ." "But
    Mellow's intention is not criticism but biography."

8. Donald Sutherland. See II-E-xlviii-2.

    "In many ways the work [*Charmed Circle*] is a triumph, and
    ought to be definitive, but it has its shortcomings, some serious
    and some not." The facts are "at least approximately correct."

9. Baker, Carlos. "A Rose for a Rose for a Rose."
   Commonweal, 100 (12 July 1974), 386-88.

    One wonders why Baker bothered to review Mellow.

10. Patricia Beer. See II-E-xlviii-3.

    Mellow's is "a variorum edition of all these events"; he does
    not give his opinions.

11. Earl Fendelman. See II-F-ix-6.

Mellow provides "aesthetic ground, that is lacking in Bridgman." He is good in creating a sense of milieu; bad in "that he does not particularly care for what Gertrude Stein wrote."

12. Hoffman, Michael J. "*Charmed Circle: Gertrude Stein and Company.*" *Journal of Modern Literature*, 4, No. 5 (1975 supplement), 1117-18.

Mellow is weak on the literary side; he has written a successful " 'life' rather than a successful literary biography." It is the best " 'life' " yet.

"To see Stein as the center of a 'charmed circle' is perhaps valid, but only in a limited sense. She was a highly gregarious person around whom many leading artists circled. But she was also a solitary figure who for years had so much difficulty in publishing her works soon after they were written that she developed primarily alone. The charmed circle of the mandala that Stein used on her stationery does symbolize this side of Stein, the most important side of her life for those of us who enjoy her writings. The life of Stein in this 'charmed circle' has yet to be written."

xiv. **Janet Hobhouse.** *Everybody Who Was Anybody* (I-B-i-7)

1. Bridgman, Richard. Review of *Everybody Who Was Anybody*. *American Literature*, 48 (1976/77), 401.

2. David Carter. See I-F-ix-1.

Hobhouse "adds little to our knowledge . . . apart from being rather more explicit about the lesbian influences around Miss Stein at college, and about the lifelong relationship with Alice Toklas. As a superficial description of where she lived and what she did, it is readable, well illustrated, thorough and well documented. As an attempt to understand another human being and a puzzling writer it is lamentable."

xv. Carolyn Faunce Copeland. *Language and Time and
Gertrude Stein* (II-A-4)

1. Holman, C. Hugh. Review of *Language and Time and
Gertrude Stein*. *American Literature*, 48 (1976/77), 605-06.

G. Books Containing Some of the Aforementioned Articles

1. Cerf, Bennett. "Stein Song." *Try and Stop Me.* New York: Simon and Schuster, 1944. Pp. 128-31.

   Appeared, somewhat altered, in "Trade Winds," (I-B-iii-18).

2. Fadiman, Clifton. *Appreciations: Essays.* Sel. by Peter Green. London: Hodder and Stoughton, 1962.

   Appreciation essays were taken from *Any Number Can Play* and *Party of One* (World Pub., 1955). "Gertrude Stein," pp. 97-107, originally appeared in *Party of One*, and is a history of Fadiman's many Stein reviews, which he frequently excerpts. II-E-xi-4, II-E-xvii-1, and II-E-xxiii-1 appear. Stein is the lady he would "most dread being cast upon a desert island with." "Gertrude Stein" follows the pattern of all of Fadiman's reviews, with the exception of the following statement: "I can only account for the effect she appears to have had on many talented writers by citing, first, the feverishly experimental literary climate of the twenties when novelty was almost always given a warmer welcome than sanity, and, second, the youthfulness of her then devotees."
   Fadiman quotes Georges Braque et al. (II-C-42) to try to support his contentions against Stein and *Autobiography*.

3. Flanner, Janet. *Paris Was Yesterday (1925-1939).* Ed. Irving Drutman. New York: Popular Library, ca. 1972.

   Among the "Letter from Paris" essays included are those on *Autobiography of Alice B. Toklas, The Relation of Human Nature to Human Life; Or the Geographical History of the United States* [sic], and Stein's move to Rue Christine.

4. Gass, William H. *Fiction and the Figures of Life.* New York: Vintage Books, 1972.

   "Gertrude Stein: Her Escape from Protective Language" is reprinted here with, however, more explanatory footnotes than the original article.

5. Heissenbüttel, Helmut. *Über Literatur: Aufsätze und Frankfurter Vorlesungen.* Olten: Walter-Verlag, 1966.

   "Reduzierte Sprache: Über einen Text von Gertrude Stein," pp. 9-19, is reprinted.

6. Porter, Katherine Anne. *The Days Before.* London: Secker and Warburg, 1953.

   "Gertrude Stein: Three Views" consists of "Everybody Is a Real One" (II-E-v-4), "Second Wind" (II-E-vii-1) and "Wooden Umbrella."

7. ———. *The Collected Essays and Occasional Writings of Katherine Anne Porter.* New York: Delacorte Press, 1970.

   The three articles mentioned above and "Ole Woman River: A Correspondence with Katherine Anne Porter" appear.

8. Riding, Laura. *Contemporaries and Snobs.* New York: Doubleday, Doran, 1928.

   "T. E. Hulme, the New Barbarism, and Gertrude Stein" appear between pp. 123 and 199.

9. Rosenberg, Harold. "Paris Annexed." *The Re-Definition of Art: Action Art to Pop to Earthworks.* London: Secker and Warburg, 1972. Pp. 167-77.

   Rosenberg's book contains articles on Jean Arp, Jean Debuffet, earthworks, Piet Mondrian, Roy Lichtenstein, Claes Oldenburg, and, in Chapter 15, "Four Americans in Paris." "Perhaps even more than the painters, [Mike, Leo and Sarah] lived in the reflection of the works they collected. But not Gertrude Stein, who, as everyone knows, lived in her own reflection." He includes some biographical information on the Steins, and devotes a large section to Stein's art criticism and to *Picasso.* "With Cubism, as Gertrude understood it, aesthetics had become irrelevant. Or a new aesthetics had been promulgated, based on the exclusion of artifice."

10. Williams, William Carlos. *Autobiography*. New York: New Directions, 1951.

   This contains, along with innumerable references, the essay "Gertrude Stein," which mostly concerns having tea with Stein and Alice B. Toklas in 1927. This leads into a discussion of "words and words," in which Williams quotes his "Work of Gertrude Stein"; Laurence Sterne's discussion of words in *Tristram Shandy* (Chapter 43) was a direct forerunner of Stein (especially *Geography and Plays*).

11. ———. *Selected Essays*. New York: Random House, 1954.

   "The Work of Gertrude Stein" and "A 1 Pound Stein" is included.

H. Miscellaneous Mentions

1. Michaud, Regis. *The American Novel Today: A Social and Psychological Study*. Boston: Little, Brown and Co., 1928.

2. Bacon, Peggy. "Facts about Faces: VI. Gertrude Stein." *New Republic*, 82 (13 March 1935), 120.
   Here appears a sketch of Gertrude Stein, accompanied by a description of the sketch, by Peggy Bacon.

3. Bodenheim, Maxwell. "To Gertrude Stein." *Poetry: A Magazine of Verse*, 57 (December 1940), 193.

4. Kazin, Alfred. *On Native Grounds: An Interpretation of Modern American Literature*. New York: Harcourt, Brace and Co., 1942.

5. Harper, Allanah. "A Magazine and Some People in Paris." *Partisan Review*, 9 (July-August 1942), 316.
   Harper includes a brief mention of Stein and her art collection.

6. Rönnebeck, Arnold. "Gertrude Was Always Giggling." *Books Abroad*, 19 (Winter 1945), 3-7.
   Rönnebeck reminisces about Stein, Pablo Picasso and others he knew in Paris, 1912-13. He sees Stein's work as "photographic."

7. Hoffman, Frederick J. *The Little Magazine: A History and a Bibliography*. Princeton: Princeton University Press, 1946.

8. Kimball, Fisher. "Matisse: Recognition, Patronage, Collecting." *Philadelphia Museum Bulletin*, 217 (March 1948), 34-47.
   Written by the director of the Philadelphia Museum—in which a future Henri Matisse exhibition would take place— this article attempts to relate the history of the Stein collection

with the individual pictures by Matisse. Gertrude is
mentioned a few times.

9. McAfee, Tom. "Gertrude Stein." *Prairie Schooner*, 32
(Spring 1948), 14.

   This poem is in honor of Stein and celebrates her
   experiments with language.

10. Toklas, Alice B. "They Who Came to Paris to
Write." *New York Times*, 6 August 1950, Sec. 7, pp. 1
and 25.

   This is subtitled "Impressions, Observations and Asides
   by Gertrude Stein's Closest Companion."

11. Hoffman, Frederick J. *The Modern Novel in America:
1900-1950*. Chicago: Henry Regnery, 1951.

   Chapter 4 is entitled "Gertrude Stein: The Method and the
   Subject." Hoffman writes about Stein's theory of composition
   which insists "upon the thing seen, or felt, or experienced."
   "Like the cautionary discipline of imagism in poetry, Miss
   Stein's explanation and practice could make an excellent but
   a limited contribution to modern writing; it could point to an
   indispensable minimum of the art, but there remained other
   disciplines of mind and imagination which depended upon an
   individual writer's capacity for developing."

12. MacShane, Frank. "Transatlantic Review." *London
Magazine*, 7, No. 12 (December 1960), 49-59.

   MacShane relates the history of *Transatlantic Review* and the
   part it played in various careers—those of Ford Madox
   Ford, Ernest Hemingway, Stein (who was a shareholder), and so on.

13. Feibleman, James K. "Literary New Orleans between
World Wars." *Southern Review*, New Series 1, No. 3
(Summer 1965), 702-19.

   Feibleman dined with Stein in New Orleans.

14. Wyatt, Sophia. "Gertrude and the Real Bobolink." *Manchester Guardian*, 9 June 1966, p. 8.

Wyatt seems to have visited Robert Bartlett Haas in California; she saw the house and Stein manuscripts. Haas discovered Stein by scanning the Cumulative Index; it was an affair "carried on entirely by correspondence."

Haas had originally planned a "Primer" with Stein which "would trace her literary development in phases with introductions by friends—Thornton Wilder on 'Plays', Pablo Picasso on 'Portraits', and Edith Sitwell on 'Poetry'. The plan became so unwieldy that it folded."

15. Porter, Katherine Anne. "Ole Woman River." *Sewanee Review*, 74, No. 3 (Summer 1966), 754-67.

16. Perrine, Lawrence. "Frost's 'The Rose Family'." *Explicator*, 26, No. 5 (January 1968), No. 43.

Perrine refers to "the faintest echo of Gertrude Stein's famous line" as one of two literary allusions in Robert Frost's poem.

17. Marks, J. "The New Humor." *Esquire*, 72, No. 6 (December 1969), 218-20+.

Marks refers to Stein as one of the "promulgators of the put-on" (example, *Autobiography of Alice B. Toklas*), "but stoned humor also found its beginnings in surrealism and in Stein's nonobjective language, like *Four Saints in Three Acts* or *Have They Attacked Mary. He Giggled (A Political Caricature)*."

18. Hamilton, George Heard. "Art: Pre-Columbian to Pinstripe." *Saturday Review*, 53 (28 November 1970), 41-43.

Hamilton mentions *Gertrude Stein on Picasso*.

19. Fisher, Edward. "Lost Generations, Then and Now." *Connecticut Review*, 6, No. 1 (1973), 13-25.

III. Indexes

Note: A bold face number in an entry (as I-A-i-**12**)
indicates authorsip or editorship of an entry; a light
face number (as I-B-i-12) indicates mention in the
amnotation.

A. Index of Names

Frieling, Kenneth II-C-**202**
Frost, Robert II-H-16
Fuller, Edmind I-B-ii-**88**
Futurists I-B-ii-70; II-B-17; II-C-11

Gagey, Edmond M. II-C-**81**
Gallup, Donald I-A-i-**4**; I-B-i-**5**; I-B-iii-**33**, **78**; II-C-**83**,
    86, **89**, **93**, **102**, **107**, 140, **163**; II-D-**14**, **16**;
    II-E-xlv-1; II-F-iii
Garvin, Harry Raphael II-B-**10**; II-C-**109**, **115**, **185**
Gass, William H. II-C-**122**, **191**, **192**; II-D-**25**; II-G-**4**
Geismar, Maxwell II-F-iii-**3**
Genêt see Flanner
George, Jonathan C. II-C-**189**
Gerstenberger, Donna I-A-i-**2**
Gervasi, Frank I-B-iii-**74**
Gillespie, A. Lincoln, Jr. I-B-ii-**38**
Gilot, Françoise I-B-ii-**39**
Glasgow, Ellen I-B-ii-**40**; I-B-iii-**44**
Glasco, John I-B-ii-**41**
Gloster, Hugh M. II-C-**84**
Glueck, Grace I-B-iii-**58**, **60**, **62**, **63**
Gold, Arthur I-B-iii-**91**
Gold, Michael II-C-**45**, **67**
Goldstein, Malcolm, I-B-ii-**42**
Golson, Lucille M. II-A-**5**
Gordon, Irene II-A-**5**; II-C-**161**, 170; II-F-x
Gorman, Herbert II-E-xviii-**4**
Gotham Book Mart I-A-i-**3**
Grace, Harvey I-B-ii-**43**
Gramont, Elisabeth de I-B-ii-12
Graves, Robert II-C-7, **15**
Gray, James II-E-xxvi-**3**
Green, Peter II-G-**2**

Russell, Francis II-A-**14**; II-F-iv-**4**

ECS II-E-xviii-**5**
Saarinen, Aline B. I-B-iii-**38**, **39**
Salmon, André II-C-**42**
Sappho II-C-155
Saroyan, William II-F-iii-**6**
Sawyer, Julian I-A-i-**5**; I-A-ii-**1**, **2**; II-A-9; II-C-**75**
Sayre, Henry Marshall II-B-**19**
Schlauch, Margaret II-C-**72**
Schmalhausen, Samuel D. II-C-**17**
Shcmitt-von Mühlenfels, Franz II-C-**213**
Schmitz, Neil II-C-**198**
Shcneider, Isidor II-C-**35**
Schneps, Maurice I-B-ii-**77**
Schorer, Mark II-C-**157**
Schwartz, Harry W. I-A-i-**6**
Schwartz, Marvin II-C-176
Scott, Winfield Townley II-F-iii-**2**; II-F-vi-**5**
Secrest, Meryle I-B-ii-**78**
Sedgwick, Ellery II-C-107
Seroff, Victor I-B-ii-**79**
Sevareid, Eric I-B-ii-**80**; I-B-iii-74
Shapiro, Harriet II-C-**181**
Shapiro, Karl II-E-xxxvii-**4**
Shattuck, Roger I-B-ii-**81**, **82**; II-F-vi-**2**
Shaw, Burnett I-B-iii-**49**
Shaw, Sharon II-C-**197**
Sherman, Stuart P. II-E-iii-**5**
Shirley, David L. I-B-iii-**95**
Shults, Donald II-C-**154**
Sievers, W. David II-C-**111**
Simon, Linda I-B-i-**13**, **14**
Simon, Robert A. II-E-xxvii-**1**

B. Index of Stein's Works